A DISCIPLESHIP JOURNEY FOR INDIVIDUALS, SMALL GROUPS, AND CONGREGATIONS

ROOTED IN DISCIPLESHIP

CULTIVATING A LIFE OF PRAYER, PRESENCE, GIFTS, SERVICE, AND WITNESS

JEFFERSON M. FURTADO

ROOTED IN DISCIPLESHIP

Copyright © 2025 by Jefferson M. Furtado
Publisher Minister's Helper
ISBN 979-8-9937666-2-1 (Physical)

All rights reserved. No part of this publication may be reproduced, distributed, or transmitted in any form or by any means, including photocopying, recording, or other electronic or mechanical methods, without the prior written permission of the publisher, except in the case of brief quotations embodied in critical reviews and certain other noncommercial uses permitted by copyright law.

Scripture quotations in this book are taken from the following Bible translations:

Common English Bible (CEB).
Copyright © 2011 by Common English Bible.
Used by permission. All rights reserved.

English Standard Version® (ESV®).
Copyright © 2001 by Crossway, a publishing ministry of Good News Publishers.
Used by permission. All rights reserved.

NET Bible® (NET).
Copyright © 1996–2019 by Biblical Studies Press, L.L.C.
www.netbible.com
All rights reserved.

New Revised Standard Version (NRSV).
Copyright © 1989 by the Division of Christian Education of the National Council of the Churches of Christ in the U.S.A.
Used by permission. All rights reserved.

New Revised Standard Version, Updated Edition (NRSVUE).
Copyright © 2021 by the National Council of the Churches of Christ in the United States of America.
Used by permission. All rights reserved.

To my wife, the Rev. Linda Louise Furtado—my best friend, fiercest critic, deepest encourager, and wisest counselor—for twenty years of unwavering love, patience, and partnership in life and ministry.

To our daughters—Sueli Renée, Cíntia Marie, and Emma Luíza—who daily teach me the meaning, depth, and joy of love, and whose lives remind me of God's goodness and grace.

To my parents, the Rev. José Magalhães Furtado and Sueli Rocha Furtado, who planted and watered in me the seeds of love for God, for people, and for learning.

To my sisters:

- *The Rev. Lady Glória Magalhães Furtado Nunes, whose theological wisdom and love for God inspire my journey.*

- *Cintia Magalhães Listenbee, whose faith, discipleship, and mastery of language have shaped both this work and my life.*

- *Simone Furtado Gray, whose groundedness in life's realities keeps me honest and calls me beyond the safety of academic circles into the urgency of real life.*

To my in-laws, the Rev. Shirley Renée Franklin and Victor Leon Franklin, Sr., whose steadfast love and guidance have been a blessing throughout my journey.

And in memory of my grandmothers, Maria da Glória Inácio Furtado and Lady de Souza Rocha, whose pioneering and evangelistic spirits continue to inspire me and call me forward in faith.

CONTENTS

PART 1   Introduction: An Invitation to Discipleship............ 1

    Getting Started: Discipleship as a Way of Life... 5
    Going Deeper: Living the Vows with Intention 7
    Self-Assessment: Where Are You in Your Discipleship Journey? 10
    Results & Growth Recommendations.. 11
    Next Steps & Faith Action Plan 11
    Discipleship Practice Matrix Description 12

PART 2   Prayers: Cultivating Communion with God 17

    Introduction 17
    Developing a Life of Prayer 18
    How to Pray 20
    Praying the Psalms.. 24
    Types of Prayers 30

PART 3   Presence: Being Fully Present in Community ... 35

    Introduction 35
    What is Worship? 38
    Why Do We Worship?... 41
    Being Present in Worship 44
    The Ways We Worship 46
    Small Groups and Fellowship 48
    Showing Up for One Another 52

PART 4   Gifts: Generosity as an Act of Worship................ 57

    Introduction 57

    Money Matters 59
    Our Spiritual Gifts..63
    What's That in Your Hand? 67
    Identifying our Gifts and Talents...71
    Gifts of the Head 72
    Gifts of the Hand 74
    Gifts of the Heart 76

PART 5 Service: Embodying Christ's Love........................... 79
    Introduction...79
    Service As Wesleyan Discipleship..81
    A Trinitarian Framework for Service 86
    Three Arenas of Service: In-Church, Local Outreach, and Global Mission 87
    Formation through Service 90
    Reflection as a Spiritual Discipline 93

PART 6 Witness: Sharing Our Faith Boldly 97
    Introduction...97
    Sharing Our Faith – The Verbal Witness 99
    Living Out Our Faith: The Embodied Witness............................104
    Practices That Form a Public Faith 107
    Community and Global Witness 110
    A Structure of Nurture, Outreach, and Witness........................114
    Outreach: Serving Beyond Ourselves...115
    Witness: Sharing God's Love 116
    A Journey for Every Generation 117

GLOSSARY 118

APPENDIX 1: Faith Story Workshop:
                "Telling Our Story, Sharing God's Grace" 123
    Workshop Overview:..123
    Workshop Outline 124
    Faith Story Toolkit 127

> So live in Christ Jesus the Lord in the same way as you received him. ⁷ Be rooted and built up in him, be established in faith, and overflow with thanksgiving just as you were taught.
>
> COLOSSIANS 2:6-7 (CEB)

FORWARD
A Shared Journey of Grace

Somewhere between the ages of eight and ten, I found myself accompanying my paternal grandmother on a church visitation. Growing up in a Methodist Church in Brazil, such visits were a familiar rhythm of congregational life. It was a Monday afternoon—the day set aside for visiting new converts after the Sunday service. My grandmother, a circle of faithful women from the church, and I—for some reason, tagging along—arrived at the home of a young woman who had just given her life to Christ. I cannot recall the exact words spoken that day, but I do remember my grandmother explaining that following Jesus was a transformative experience. She also told the young woman that this new life in Christ did not mean her struggles would suddenly vanish. What it did mean, however, was that she was now part of the family of God. And as a member of this newfound family and a community of faith, she would never have to walk through the challenges of life alone again.

That simple visit remains etched in my memory, not because of the eloquence of words spoken or some grand gestures offered, but because of the profound truth it revealed: discipleship is never meant to be lived in isolation. My grandmother's assurance to that young believer was both pastoral and

FORWARD

profoundly theological—life with Christ is a gift of grace, and it is also a calling into a community where we learn, grow, struggle, and persevere together.

This memory has shaped my understanding of the Christian life. When I left home and ventured into life in the United States as an eighteen-year-old, I was still trying to figure out what it meant to be a committed follower of Christ—one who practiced faith not simply because I had been told to do so, but because it offered the lifeline I needed to thrive, even in the midst of challenges. In the years that followed, I encountered seasons of loss, unemployment, financial strain, health scares, and all the uncertainties that life inevitably brings. Through those moments, I discovered the deep necessity of remaining connected to the source of our strength and to a community of support beyond myself. Faith was no longer an inherited routine; it became a living practice that sustained me, a rhythm of grace that carried me when I could not carry myself.

John Wesley and the early Methodists understood this same reality well. They knew that faith could not be sustained by private devotion alone. This is why they gathered believers into class meetings and bands, small groups where prayer was offered, Scripture was read, gifts were discerned, service was encouraged, and witness was shared. These were not optional activities; they were the very practices that kept disciples rooted in God's grace and accountable to one another.

In the United Methodist Church today, we name these practices each time we take membership vows: prayer, presence, gifts, service, and witness. They are more than promises to keep the church functioning; they are patterns of life that form us into Christ's likeness. When we pray, we open ourselves to God's transforming Spirit. When we show up with presence, we embody faithfulness to God and neighbor. When we share our gifts, we participate in God's economy of grace. When we serve, we join in Christ's mission in the world. When we bear witness, we become living testimonies to God's love and power. Together, these vows invite us into a life of discipleship that is personal, communal, and missional.

Rooted in Discipleship grows from this conviction. It is both a workbook and a guide, but more importantly it is an invitation—a call to live our United

Methodist membership vows in ways that deepen our faith and strengthen our communities. This resource is designed to help congregations and individuals practice prayer, presence, gifts, service, and witness not as obligations, but as spiritual disciplines that cultivate holiness of heart and life. In a time when faith is too easily reduced to programs or fragmented into occasional events, this work reminds us that discipleship is a way of life. It is daily, communal, and sustained by practices that root us in the love of God and empower us to bear fruit for the sake of the world.

Now the eleven disciples went to Galilee, to the mountain where Jesus told them to go. When they saw him, they worshipped him, but some doubted. Jesus came near and spoke to them, "I've received all authority in heaven and on earth. Therefore, go and make disciples of all nations, baptizing them in the name of the Father and of the Son and of the Holy Spirit, teaching them to obey everything that I've commanded you. Look, I myself will be with you every day until the end of this present age.

Matthew 28:16-20 (CEB)

PART 1
INTRODUCTION
An Invitation to Discipleship

"Go therefore and make disciples of all nations…" (Matthew 28:19, CEB). With these words, Jesus entrusted to His followers a mission that remains central to the life and work of the Church today. Discipleship is not an optional endeavor for the committed few but the heart of Christian identity and purpose. This project emerges as both a theological conviction and a pastoral response to the discipleship crisis facing today's Church. It seeks to recover, reframe, and renew the Church's commitment to intentional discipleship, rooted in the Wesleyan tradition and embodied in the life of local congregations. It offers a bold, Spirit-led framework grounded in Wesleyan practice and deeply attuned to the challenges and longings of contemporary congregational life.

This work emerges out of a desire to cultivate a discipleship system that is not merely programmatic but theological, pastoral, and transformative. What distinguishes this framework is its unapologetic insistence that discipleship must be more than programming—it must become a way of life, deeply embedded in the rhythms of grace. At its core, this project affirms that discipleship is the essence of the Church's mission and the lifeblood of Christian community. It

ROOTED IN DISCIPLESHIP

invites a shift from passive participation in church life to an active, Spirit-empowered journey of transformation and mission.

It challenges congregations to move from maintenance to mission, from content consumption to spiritual cultivation. The Great Commission given in Matthew 28 is not only a missional mandate but a pastoral framework for forming followers of Jesus who reflect God's love, mercy, and justice in the world.

Within this framework, the United Methodist Church offers a distinct expression of discipleship through its membership vows: prayers, presence, gifts, service, and witness. These vows are not a nostalgic nod to tradition—they are vibrant, countercultural habits that can renew the Church's witness in a fractured world.

Vows are more than liturgical moments as congregations receive new persons into church membership; they are a rule of life for the people called Methodists. These five commitments offer a theological and practical foundation for cultivating a holistic discipleship system that is sustainable, reproducible, and transformative. Each vow represents a particular dimension of faithful living. Together, these five practices reflect a dynamic and grace-filled pattern of discipleship that shapes both individual lives and communal witness.

In United Methodist congregations across diverse contexts, there is an urgent need to reclaim these vows as intentional practices for spiritual formation.[1] This project dares to ask: What if the vows we recite at baptism and membership became the actual blueprint for our spiritual growth?

Too often, discipleship is either reduced to church attendance or confined to isolated educational programs. This project challenges that paradigm by proposing a shift toward discipleship as a way of life.

It invites clergy and laity alike to revisit the theological roots of our Wesleyan heritage, to rekindle the communal and personal rhythms of holiness that defined the early Methodist movement, and to respond to God's grace with lives marked by faith in action.

This project is organized around three central convictions:

> ➢ **Discipleship is transformational:** It is the process by which we are formed in the image of Christ for the sake of the world. It involves both inward transformation—the renewing of our minds, hearts, and

INTRODUCTION

desires—and outward expression—embodying the love, compassion, and justice of Christ in every dimension of life.

> **Discipleship is intentional:** It requires structure, commitment, and accountability. Just as the early Methodists organized themselves into class meetings and bands for mutual support and growth, this book argues for a discipleship system that cultivates rhythms of engagement, reflection, and spiritual discipline. Growth in grace does not happen by accident; it requires an intentional posture toward God and neighbor.

> **Discipleship is holistic:** It engages the entire person—heart, mind, body, and spirit. Through prayer, presence, gifts, service, and witness, disciples live into a fully embodied faith that touches every part of life. Holistic discipleship connects spiritual practices with practical application, theological reflection with daily living.

Each chapter of this project explores one of the membership vows as a distinct yet interconnected pathway for discipleship.

These vows function not as checkboxes to be completed, but as spiritual disciplines that help form Christlike character. Each section includes theological grounding, historical Methodist context, practical guidance, and reflective questions for personal or communal engagement.

The chapter on prayer invites disciples to develop consistent, honest, and Spirit-led communication with God. Drawing on biblical examples, Wesleyan practice, and diverse prayer forms, it presents prayer as the foundational practice of the Christian life.

The chapter on presence calls attention to the incarnational nature of Christian community and the role of corporate worship as a means of grace. It emphasizes the spiritual importance of showing up—for God, for others, and for the work of the church.

The chapter on gifts reframes stewardship as a joyful response to grace—not a burdensome obligation, but a spiritual discipline that reflects God's generosity. It explores financial giving, vocational calling, and the use of personal skills for the building up of the body of Christ.

The chapter on service explores how acts of compassion and justice form the core of Christian witness. Drawing from the life of Jesus and the example of John Wesley, it emphasizes serving the last, the least, and the lost.

ROOTED IN DISCIPLESHIP

The final vow, witness, challenges disciples to live out and share the gospel through word and deed. In a time when Christianity is often associated with institutional decline or cultural entrenchment, reclaiming authentic Christian witness rooted in love, humility, and courage is essential. This section connects evangelism with storytelling, justice, and prophetic presence in the world.

The theological insights of John and Charles Wesley, particularly their understanding of grace—prevenient, justifying, and sanctifying—undergird the vision of this work. Discipleship, from a Wesleyan perspective, is always a response to God's initiative, always empowered by the Spirit, and always directed toward love of God and neighbor.

This project also includes a practical component: a suggested discipleship rhythm or matrix that individuals and churches can use to track and deepen their spiritual practices. Rather than offering rigid prescriptions, this framework encourages congregations to discern practices that are Spirit-led, context-sensitive, and missionally faithful.

The framework encourages reflection on frequency (daily, weekly, monthly, etc.) and alignment of personal habits with communal values.

Finally, this project recognizes that discipleship cannot be reduced to individualistic spirituality. It is deeply communal. Wesley's insistence that there is no holiness but social holiness calls the church to engage *discipleship as a shared journey. Wesley's enduring insistence that "there is no holiness but social holiness" reminds us that discipleship is not a private affair, but a shared journey into the heart of Go*The goal is not merely to make converts, but to nurture committed followers of Jesus who embody the gospel in every aspect of life.

In a world marked by spiritual hunger, division, and injustice, the Church is called to embody a different way—the way of Christ. This book is offered as a contribution to that work. It is an invitation to rediscover the power of intentional, grace-filled discipleship within the life of the church. It is a call to deepen our walk with Christ, to renew our commitment to community, and to offer our lives in witness to the transforming love of God.

May this work serve as both inspiration and guide for churches seeking to live more fully into their identity as communities of discipleship, grounded in grace and sent into the world to be light, salt, and leaven in the name of Jesus Christ.

INTRODUCTION

Getting Started: Discipleship as a Way of Life

In the life of the Church, vows are not casual promises or symbolic gestures. They are sacred commitments—covenants made in the presence of God and the gathered community that bind us to a particular way of life. To take a vow is to say with reverence and resolve, "I intend, by the grace of God, to order my life according to the gospel." Christian vows are not merely about obligation; they are about orientation. They shape our lives toward God, anchor us in community, and set us on a journey of transformation.

In the Wesleyan tradition, vows serve a vital role in our ongoing sanctification. John Wesley believed that grace is not static—it moves. It stirs. It draws us deeper into the life of God and sends us outward into love of neighbor. The membership vows of The United Methodist Church—prayers, presence, gifts, service, and witness—are concrete ways we respond to that grace. They are not prerequisites for salvation, but responses to it. They are not abstract ideals, but embodied practices that help form us into people of faith, love, and justice.

These vows emerge from and reaffirm our baptismal identity. When we enter into membership in a local church, we are not joining a club; we are entering a covenant. This covenant expresses our desire to live as disciples of Jesus Christ, to be nurtured and held accountable by a community of faith, and to commit ourselves to the mission of God in the world. Vows give shape to that covenant. They tell us what it means to live baptized—to live as people who belong to God and to one another.

Yet in many places, the power and purpose of these vows have been diminished or forgotten. Too often, church membership is treated as a formality—an entry point into institutional life rather than an initiation into a rule of life. But when rightly understood and intentionally practiced, these vows offer far more. They provide a spiritual rhythm that grounds us, challenges us, and sustains us. They are habits of grace that open us to the transforming work of the Holy Spirit.

Why, then, should one be eager to take these vows? Because they are invitations. They invite us to a life of purpose, accountability, and joy. In a fragmented and often rootless world, they offer direction and depth. In a culture of individualism, they call us into shared life. In the face of suffering and injustice, they mold us to be people of compassion, courage, and hope. These vows are not burdens to carry but pathways to life. They draw us into deeper communion with God, stronger connection with others, and fuller participation in God's redemptive work.

ROOTED IN DISCIPLESHIP

Each vow—prayers, presence, gifts, service, and witness—shapes a particular dimension of discipleship. But they are not isolated. They work together, forming a whole pattern of Christian life that is holistic, sustainable, and Spirit-filled. They are tools of spiritual formation and marks of faithful living. And when embraced fully, they lead us into the joy of knowing Christ and making Christ known.

Why These Vows Still Matter Today

We live in a society that prizes autonomy, self-expression, and personal fulfillment. In this society, the idea of taking communal vows can seem countercultural—perhaps even restrictive. We live in an age that celebrates choice over commitment, freedom over formation, and the self over the community. In such a world, promises are often provisional, and identity is self-constructed rather than covenantally received. It is precisely in this cultural moment, however, that the vows of church membership become more—not less—relevant.

These vows offer a needed corrective to the isolation and instability that mark so much of modern life. Where individualism says, "I'll go at it alone," vows say, "I will walk this path with others." Where consumerism says, "I will participate if it meets my needs," vows say, "I will serve even when it costs me." Where cultural transience says, "I'll stay as long as it's convenient," vows say, "I belong here, and I am accountable to this community." In a world of temporary commitments and ever-shifting loyalties, these promises become anchors—rooting us in God's story, Christ's body, and the Spirit's mission.

To take vows in the Church today is a prophetic act. It is to reject the notion that faith is a private affair, detached from others and shaped solely by personal preference. It is to affirm that discipleship is relational, accountable, and embodied in community. Vows draw us out of ourselves and into a shared life where grace is both given and received. They remind us that we are not just spiritual consumers but covenant partners in God's redemptive work.

Moreover, the vows invite us into habits that cultivate a deeper, more resilient faith. In a culture of distraction, prayer grounds us. In a society of superficial connection, presence binds us. In a world of scarcity and self-preservation, generosity frees us. In a time of injustice and despair, service and witness become signs of God's kingdom breaking into the present.

4These practices endure not because they are traditional, but because they are transformational. They offer an alternative to the thinness of self-centered

INTRODUCTION

spirituality. They point us beyond ourselves toward the greater purposes of God. In doing so, they shape us into the kind of people the world desperately needs—people of hope, integrity, humility, and holy love.

If these vows shape us into people of hope and love, how do we begin to live them out? In what ways do they guide our everyday discipleship?

The five membership vows of The United Methodist Church—prayers, presence, gifts, service, and witness—offer more than moral encouragement; they form a spiritual pathway. Practiced with intention, these vows become a framework by which we grow in grace, deepen in faith, and participate in God's transforming work in the world. Each vow opens a doorway into a particular dimension of Christian living, yet they are meant to be practiced together, as part of a shared and holistic way of life.

To explore these vows meaningfully, we must first return to a deeper understanding of *what discipleship truly is*. For discipleship is the larger calling—the journey into which these vows invite us. It is the soil in which the vows take root and bear fruit.

Going Deeper: Living the Vows with Intention
So What Is Discipleship?

Discipleship is more than simply attending church services or knowing the Scriptures. While these are important for the life of faith, discipleship calls us to a lifelong journey of growing deeper in our relationship with God and embodying the teachings of Jesus in every aspect of our lives. As United Methodists, we believe that discipleship requires intentionality, dedication, and a willingness to engage fully with our faith through action. Our membership vows—prayers, presence, gifts, service, and witness—serve as the guideposts for this journey, helping us to live out our faith in tangible, meaningful ways.

The call to discipleship is an invitation to go deeper in our walk with Christ—to move beyond the surface and cultivate a faith that is active, dynamic, and transformative. This is a type of work that matures with us, a way of life that grows as we grow. It allows us to engage the complexities of our lives with grace and clarity, because, as the great theologian Howard Thurman reminds us, "Life is alive, complex, and dynamic."[2] The vows help us meet life with a faith that is equally alive—grounded in Christ and animated by the Spirit.

Whether we spend intentional time in prayer, show up for others in times of need, offer our gifts and talents to support the church's mission, serve our neighbors, or boldly share the message of the gospel, each of these practices shapes us into the likeness of Christ and reflects God's love to the world.

Going deeper means recognizing that these vows are not individual checkboxes but interconnected elements of a holistic faith. As we grow in one area—such as prayer or service—it strengthens our capacity to live out the other vows as well. Each step in our discipleship journey brings us closer to God, empowers us to serve others fully, and strengthens our community of faith. Through this process, we become vessels of God's grace, embodying the love of Christ in all that we do.

Discipleship requires both commitment and vulnerability, as it challenges us to examine our hearts, grow in humility, and continually strive toward spiritual maturity. As you engage with these vows, remember that you do not walk this path alone. You are part of a community that supports and encourages you—journeying together toward a deeper, more vibrant faith.

We cannot speak about practice without speaking of intentionality. An intentional process helps us develop consistency in our efforts to grow in faith. As we grow, we can cultivate meaningful prayer practices that foster deeper connection with God. We can move from being merely physically present in worship and community events to being mentally and emotionally engaged. We can reflect on how our financial resources, time, and talents might serve the mission of the Church, directing our spiritual gifts and passions toward serving others in impactful ways. And we can consider how our faith journey might move toward outward witness—sharing our story and embodying the gospel in everyday life.

Maturing in our faith development, means to naturally weave reflection and action together. This blend equips us to live out our faith authentically, helping others see Christ through our actions and words. Through this holistic approach, we embody God's love and grace in ways that transform both ourselves and the world around us.

The Five Practices of Membership: A Discipleship Framework

Before we explore each vow in depth, the following brief overview offers a working definition of the five practices. These descriptions serve as guideposts for our journey—anchoring us in grace, pointing us toward growth, and inviting us into the kind of Christian life that reflects the love and mission of Jesus Christ.

INTRODUCTION

PRAYERS: Cultivating Communion with God

Prayer is the cornerstone of our relationship with God. It is both personal and communal, shaping our inner lives and connecting us with God's will. As we pray for ourselves, the Church, and the world, we participate in God's mission and open ourselves to transformation. Prayer is one of the "means of grace" that John Wesley identified as essential for spiritual growth.

PRESENCE: Being Fully Present in Community

Presence calls us to more than physical attendance. It invites us to be emotionally and spiritually engaged in the life of the Church. Worship, small groups, and ministry life offer opportunities for deep connection, accountability, and encouragement as we grow together in faith.

GIFTS: Generosity as an Act of Worship

Our gifts—time, talents, and financial resources—are offerings of gratitude to God. Stewardship is not a burden, but a joyful response to God's grace. Through generous giving, we support the Church's mission and share in God's work of transformation.

SERVICE: Embodying Christ's Love

Following Jesus means serving others with compassion and humility. Service extends beyond programs to encompass every part of our lives. As we serve the least, the last, and the lost, we reflect Christ's love and join Him in the work of healing and justice.

WITNESS: Sharing Our Faith Boldly

Our lives are testimonies of God's grace. Witness involves both word and action—living in a way that invites others to know Christ. In a world longing for hope, our witness becomes a light that points to God's love, redemption, and truth.

Where Am I on the Journey? Tools for Reflection and Growth

Discipleship is a lifelong journey. Like any trip, stopping now and then helps. Ask yourself: Where am I right now? What direction am I headed? Where is God inviting me next?

The following tools—a self-assessment and a discipleship matrix—are offered not as tests or requirements, but as invitations. They are not about measuring performance, but about cultivating awareness. These practices are meant to

ROOTED IN DISCIPLESHIP

help you reflect on your current experiences and commitments, and to consider how God might be shaping you through the vows of prayer, presence, gifts, service, and witness.

The self-assessment can help you identify your current season of faith. The discipleship matrix offers simple, tangible practices that can be used to plan your next faithful steps. Some may use these tools to look back and reflect; others may use them to look ahead and set intentions for growth. Both are valid, grace-filled approaches. The goal is not perfection, but orientation—to turn our lives more fully toward the love, presence, and purposes of God.

Self-Assessment: Where Are You in Your Discipleship Journey?

For each question, choose the response that best reflects your experience.

1. My Relationship with God
- **A.** I am curious about faith, but unsure how to begin.
- **B.** I believe in Jesus and I am starting to grow spiritually.
- **C.** I actively pray and study Scripture to deepen my faith.
- **D.** My faith is central to my life, and I help others grow.

2. My Participation in Worship & Community
- **A.** I attend worship occasionally or not at all.
- **B.** I attend worship regularly but feel I could be more engaged.
- **C.** I participate fully in worship, small groups, and church life.
- **D.** I help lead in worship, small groups, or church ministries.

3. My Spiritual Practices
- **A.** I am unsure how to pray or read the Bible.
- **B.** I pray and read Scripture but not consistently.
- **C.** I have a regular rhythm of spiritual disciplines.
- **D.** I teach, lead, or mentor others in their spiritual growth.

4. My Engagement in Service & Outreach
- **A.** I am not yet serving in the church or community.
- **B.** I want to serve but don't know where to start.

INTRODUCTION

  C. I serve in a ministry and feel called to grow in leadership.
  D. I mentor and lead others in serving the church and world.

5. My Witness & Sharing of Faith
  A. I am not comfortable talking about my faith.
  B. I want to share my faith, but struggle to do so.
  C. I share my faith naturally through words and actions.
  D. I actively disciple and encourage others in faith.

Results & Growth Recommendations

Mostly A's → Dormant Seed (Seeking & Exploring)

Next Step: Attend worship regularly, join a group, and explore faith.

Mostly B's → Sprouting Seed (Beginning Faith)

Next Step: Deepen your spiritual practices and get involved in service.

Mostly C's → Growing Plant (Maturing Faith)

Next Step: Discover your spiritual gifts and mentor others in faith.

Mostly D's → Blossoming Plant (Bearing Fruit)

Next Step: Lead a group, disciple others, and live out your calling.

Next Steps & Faith Action Plan

Reflect on Your Growth:
- What excites you about your faith journey?
- Where do you feel God calling you to grow?
- What challenges might be holding you back?

Commit to a Next Step:
- Choose one new practice to develop in the next month.
- Find a mentor or accountability partner.
- Write a prayer of commitment to deepen your discipleship.

Connect with Others:
- Talk with a pastor or group leader about your faith journey.

ROOTED IN DISCIPLESHIP

> ➤ Join a Bible study, small group, or mission team.
> ➤ Serve in a ministry that aligns with your gifts.

Trust God's Process

Growth takes time—like a seed, faith is nurtured through prayer, learning, and community. There will be seasons of rapid growth and seasons of quiet stillness. Both are holy. Trust that even when you can't see visible change, God is at work beneath the surface, cultivating your soul with grace and preparing you for what is yet to come.

Be patient with yourself. Spiritual transformation is not about perfection, but about direction. It is the slow and steady turning of your heart toward God, again and again.

It means being honest about your doubts and your hopes, allowing God to shape you through Scripture, worship, service, and loving relationships.

Lean into community. Just as no seed grows alone, we too need others to support and encourage us.

Surround yourself with people who will pray with you, challenge you, and remind you of God's promises when you forget.

Above all, surrender the outcome to God. We plant, we water, we show up—but it is God who brings the growth.

> *"I planted, Apollos watered, but God gave the growth."*
> **- 1 CORINTHIANS 3:6, ESV.**

Let us walk this path of discipleship together with trust and humility, confident that the God who began a good work in us will carry it to completion. May we become people whose lives reflect the light, love, and grace of Jesus Christ in all we do.

Discipleship Practice Matrix Description

This matrix suggests spiritual practices aligned with the five membership vows. These are invitations to cultivate faithful rhythms, not checklists to perfect. The goal is intentional growth in grace, acknowledging that "the longest journey begins with a single step." You might choose one or two practices to focus on seasonally

INTRODUCTION

or use this matrix to reflect on your current habits. Let it be a companion to help you explore commitments, reflect deeply, and live your discipleship with greater intention—not a scorecard. What step can you begin with?

AREA	ACTION/GOAL	FREQUENCY	REFLECTION/NOTES
PRAYER	Pray at the start and end of each day	Daily	
	Pray specifically for church/community needs	Weekly	
	Keep a prayer journal to record insights	Weekly	
	Practice a new prayer form (e.g., Lectio Divina)	Monthly	
PRESENCE	Attend Sunday worship service	Weekly	
	Join a church fellowship event	Monthly	
	Connect with someone new from church	Monthly	
	Schedule a one-on-one with a spiritual mentor	Quarterly	
GIFTS	Give a tithe or offering	Weekly	
	Identify a personal skill to offer in ministry	Monthly	
	Mentor someone in an area of your expertise	Annually	
	Reflect on financial stewardship practices	Quarterly	

ROOTED IN DISCIPLESHIP

AREA	ACTION/GOAL	FREQUENCY	REFLECTION/NOTES
SERVICE	Volunteer at a church or local outreach event	Monthly	
	Commit to a specific ministry role	Weekly	
	Participate in a community service day	Quarterly	
	Identify a personal mission project	Annually	
WITNESS	Invite a friend or family member to church	Monthly	
	Share a personal testimony	Quarterly	
	Engage in conversations about faith	Weekly	
	Support an evangelism initiative	Annually	

> **REJOICE ALWAYS. PRAY CONTINUALLY. GIVE THANKS IN EVERY SITUATION BECAUSE THIS IS GOD'S WILL FOR YOU IN CHRIST JESUS.**
>
> — 1 THESSALONIANS 5:16–18 (CEB)

PART 2
PRAYERS
Cultivating Communion with God

Introduction

Our vow of prayers calls us to cultivate a life of constant connection with God. Prayer is more than a ritual; it is the foundation of our relationship with God, where we seek guidance, express gratitude, confess our struggles, and listen for God's voice.

As members of The United Methodist Church, we commit to praying for the church, its ministries, its leaders, and each other.

This chapter explores prayer as the first of five vows that shape our discipleship journey. Drawing from Scripture, Wesleyan theology, and the lived wisdom of our spiritual ancestors, we will explore personal, communal, and historical dimensions of prayer.

With practical guidance and reflection questions, this chapter invites you into a deeper, more intentional life of prayer.

ROOTED IN DISCIPLESHIP

Developing a Life of Prayer

Personal Prayer Life

Each disciple is encouraged to develop a personal prayer practice, whether through daily devotionals, quiet time, journaling, or other forms of communication with God.

Congregational Prayer

We engage in prayer as a community through Sunday worship services, small group gatherings, and special prayer meetings. These moments unite us in shared faith and reliance on God's grace.

Intercessory Prayer

We are called to pray for one another, lifting the needs of our fellow members, community, and the world. This vow reminds us that our prayers are a powerful way to support each other and bring healing and transformation.

Through prayer, we not only draw closer to God but also build a deeper sense of care and compassion for one another. Our discipleship system emphasizes regular opportunities for individual and collective prayer, creating a church culture rooted in seeking God's presence and guidance.

What is Prayer?

At its simplest, prayer is communication with God. It is how we talk to God, sharing our joys, needs, fears, and gratitude. Prayer can take many forms—silent reflection, spoken words, or even written prayers—but at its core, it is the way we connect with the divine.

Throughout the Holy Scriptures, those who walked closely with God lived lives steeped in this connection. Whether in moments of triumph or trial, they understood that dependence on God was essential for survival. Our ancestors in the faith modeled a reality that remains true today: to grow as God's people, we must stay connected to our source—God. Prayer provides us with this vital connection.

Stanley Jones, the great Methodist missionary, once said, "If I had one gift, and only one gift, to make to the Christian Church, I would offer the gift of prayer. For everything follows from prayer."[3]

PRAYERS

His words remind us that prayer—our connection with God—is the foundation that sustains the life of faith. No other practice holds the same power or effectiveness. For those of us seeking to live lives of service and community, prayer is the well from which we must continually drink if we wish to endure the long journey of discipleship.

In the Gospels, we see how essential prayer was to Jesus' life and ministry. In Luke 11:1–4, the disciples asked Jesus to teach them how to pray, and He responded by giving them the words we now know as the Lord's Prayer—a prayer that continues to shape Christian faith and practice across the world. This foundational prayer teaches us about humility, forgiveness, and trust in God's provision.

As a devout Palestinian Jew, Jesus followed a prayer practice rooted in His religious tradition, offering prayers three times a day—morning, afternoon, and evening. But prayer as a means of human connection with God began long before Jesus' time. Genesis tells us that after Adam and Eve left the Garden, "people began to invoke the name of the Lord" (Genesis 4:26, NRSVUE). As humanity began to take shape, the instinct to reach out towards God who reaches out towards was us became a defining make in the human story. Throughout the Old Testament, we encounter people and communities lifting their voices to a God who hears and responds. Prayer, then, is not just conversation but fuel for the spiritual journey—air for the soul.

Just as we depend on air to live, we also rely on prayer to sustain our spiritual lives. Breathing is an automatic process, but without it, our entire being suffers. When we inhale, we take in life-giving oxygen, and when we exhale, we release waste gasses. Similarly, prayer is a cycle of receiving and releasing. When we pray, we open ourselves to receive what is essential for our spiritual growth and release the burdens that weigh us down.

As Howard Thurman so beautifully expresses, "The things we do are an expression of our intent; our intent is the focus of our desires, and our desires are the prayers of our heart."[4] Whether we maintain a regular rhythm of prayer or turn to God in times of need, something deep within us moves us to pray—it is a spiritual instinct as natural and necessary as breathing itself.

Reflection Questions:

1. How would you describe your current prayer life?

2. Think about a time when prayer sustained you in a difficult situation. What did that experience teach you about the importance of prayer in your life?
3. Jesus taught His disciples how to pray in Luke 11:1-4. What does the Lord's Prayer mean to you? Are there specific parts of the prayer that resonate deeply with your own spiritual journey?
4. Howard Thurman says that our desires are the prayers of our heart. What are the deepest desires of your heart right now, and how do they shape your prayer life?
5. In what ways can you integrate more intentional moments of prayer into your daily routine?
6. When was the last time you prayed for someone else? How might you practice intercessory prayer more regularly, lifting others' needs before God?

How to Pray

If we understand prayer as communication with God, then the best way to learn how to pray is by simply starting that conversation. Just like any relationship, communication with God deepens through openness and practice. One of the most accessible and beautiful guides for prayer is the Book of Psalms. Often called the Bible's "Prayer Book," the Psalms provide us with a vast array of prayers and hymns composed across centuries, reflecting the spiritual life of the people of Israel.

The Psalms capture the full range of human emotions—joy, doubt, sorrow, anger, trust, and gratitude. Whether celebrating God's faithfulness, crying out for justice, or seeking comfort in times of distress, the psalms teach us that there is no emotion too big or too small to bring before God. This ancient collection witnesses to the fact that prayer is not reserved for perfect or polished words, but is the honest outpouring of our hearts to the One who listens. The poet, Kathleen Norris, said, "Prayer is not doing, but being. It is not words but the beyond-words experience of coming into the presence of something much greater than oneself.... [Prayer] is ordinary experience lived with gratitude and wonder, a wonder that makes us know the smallness of oneself in an enormous and various universe."[5]

The beauty of Psalms is that prayer doesn't have to follow a formula. It can be as simple as expressing whatever is in our hearts. Whether in moments of joy

PRAYERS

or sorrow, when we don't have the words to pray, the Psalms can serve as a guide. They offer us language for every situation, encouraging us to approach God with authenticity and trust. In teaching the disciples to pray, Jesus offered a model we can use to learn and build our own prayer.

While we recite the Lord's prayer in full, this prayer is composed of six distinct movements:

1. Start with Praise – *"Our Father who is in heaven, hallowed be your name."*

The prayer begins by praising God, recognizing His greatness and thanking Him for who He is. Before anything else, we start by honoring God. You could say something like, "God, you are good, and I thank you for being in my life."

2. Ask for God's Will – *"Your kingdom come, your will be done."*

While we have been given minds to think, hearts to feel, and the power to act, we must seek God's will for our lives and the world—not just your own. So, we ask God to help us trust His way above all else. You could say something like, "Help me trust Your plans, even when I don't understand."

3. Ask for What You Need – *"Give us today our daily bread."*

It's okay to ask for help with what you need every day, physically, emotionally, and spiritually. So bring your needs to God because God is the source of all things visible and invisible. You could say something like, "Please help me with *[specific need]* and give me strength for today."

4. Seek Forgiveness – *"Forgive us our sins as we forgive others."*

As the Apostle Paul reminds us in Romans 3:23, "All have sinned and fall short of God's glory" (CEB). So, we come to God admitting where we've made mistakes and ask God for forgiveness. We also remember to forgive others. This is a moment of confession to God. You could say something like, "I'm sorry for *[specific action]* and help me forgive others, just like you forgive me."

5. Ask for Guidance and Protection – *"Lead us not into temptation, but deliver us from evil."*

Though humanity was created in the perfect image of God, this good nature has become corrupted, and all of us are born with an inclination toward sin and rebellion against God. Charles Wesley, in his hymn, "Love Divine, All Loves Excelling," prays for God to take away our "bent" towards sinning. Here we ask God just that. We ask for help to avoid bad choices and protection from harm. You could say something like, "God, help me make wise choices and keep me safe from what's harmful."

6. End with Praise – *"For yours is the kingdom and the power and the glory."*
As with the beginning of the prayer, we close by reminding ourselves that God is in control, and give thanks not simply because we expect our requests to be fulfilled, but because we serve a God who loves us, listens, journeys with us, offers strength for the journey, and through Christ has already given us new lives. You could say something like, "Thank you, God, for all the things you do for me. In the name of Jesus. Amen."

In Matthew 6:7-8, Jesus reminds us that God is not interested in rote repetitions or an overabundance of words. God, our Heavenly Father, knows what we need before we open our mouths to ask. So, if this is your starting point, do not be concerned about feeling awkward, making mistakes, or "saying the wrong thing." God knows the intent of our hearts and listens to us. In his *Confessions*, Saint Augustine of Hippo tells us that even the desire to please God, is pleasing to Him. Augustine is teaching us that God's grace, at work in our lives, produces an inclination or desire to serve and please God, and that in itself is good. So, if you feel that you are struggling in the beginning, do not let discouragement prevent you from continuing to move forward.

Questions for Reflection and Discussion:

1. Starting the Conversation with God:
- ➤ How does viewing prayer as a conversation with God change your understanding of how to pray?
- ➤ Have you experienced times when starting a conversation with God felt natural? Or challenging? What made those moments easier or harder?

2. The Psalms as a Guide:
- ➤ The Psalms offer prayers for every emotion and situation. Is there a particular psalm that resonates with you? Why?
- ➤ How might praying through the Psalms help you bring your honest emotions—whether joy, doubt, or sorrow—before God?

PRAYERS

3. Prayer as Honest Expression:
- ➤ How does the quote from Kathleen Norris ("Prayer is not doing, but being…") challenge or affirm your understanding of what prayer should be?
- ➤ How does it feel to know that there is no emotion "too big or too small" to bring before God in prayer?

4. Learning from the Lord's Prayer:
- ➤ Jesus offered a model for prayer that includes praise, petition, forgiveness, and trust in God. Which part of this model do you find the most challenging? Why?
- ➤ How can you incorporate the movements of the Lord's Prayer—praise, asking for God's will, asking for what you need, seeking forgiveness, and asking for guidance—into your daily prayers?

5. Personalizing Prayer:
- ➤ When praying, do you find it easier to use structured prayers (like the Lord's Prayer) or more spontaneous, personal prayers? Why do you think that is?
- ➤ How might the understanding that prayer doesn't need to follow a formula help you approach God more openly?

6. Addressing Personal Needs and Seeking Forgiveness:
- ➤ What are some areas in your life where you feel the need to ask God for "daily bread" (physical, emotional, or spiritual support)?
- ➤ How does the practice of confessing your sins in prayer and forgiving others affect your relationship with God and with others?

7. Avoiding Temptation and Seeking Protection:
- ➤ In what areas of your life do you feel most in need of God's guidance and protection from harmful influences or temptations?
- ➤ How do you understand Charles Wesley's hymn lyric, "take away our bent toward sinning," in the context of your own spiritual journey?

ROOTED IN DISCIPLESHIP

8. Praise as Bookends:
- ➢ Why do you think Jesus begins and ends His model prayer with praise? How might starting and ending your prayers with praise shift your focus in prayer?
- ➢ When you praise God at the end of your prayer, are you primarily praising God for what you've asked for or for who God is?

9. Overcoming Discouragement in Prayer:
- ➢ Jesus teaches us that God knows our needs before we ask (Matthew 6:7-8). How does this change the way you approach prayer?
- ➢ Augustine teaches that even the desire to please God is pleasing to Him. How does this encourage you to keep praying, even when it feels difficult or awkward?

10. Continuing the Journey:
- ➢ How might you intentionally create space in your daily life to continue deepening your communication with God through prayer?
- ➢ What practical steps can you take this week to move forward in your prayer life, especially when you feel like you're struggling?

Praying the Psalms

Howard Thurman, a great theologian and spiritual guide, once observed that, "Human life is simple but ever complex."[6] His words speak to a reality that resonates with many of us: life can be both beautifully straightforward and overwhelmingly intricate. There are times when the complexities of our lives—whether from grief, anxiety, confusion, or weariness—become so overwhelming that we struggle to find the words to express ourselves in prayer. In moments like these, we may echo the sentiment of the writer of Ecclesiastes, who lamented, "All words are tiring; no one is able to speak. The eye isn't satisfied with seeing, neither is the ear filled up by hearing" (Ecclesiastes 1:8, CEB).

At such times, the very act of prayer may feel impossible. While we know that God, in infinite grace, understands our needs and desires before we even utter a word, there is something profoundly healing in the process of bringing those needs before God in prayer. The act of speaking—whether aloud or in the silence of our hearts—can be a path toward emotional and spiritual restoration. Yet, when our own words fail us, when our hearts feel too

PRAYERS

burdened to speak, we are not left without guidance. We can turn to the prayers of others, those who have walked the journey of faith before us and have opened themselves to God with raw honesty and vulnerability. One of the richest sources of such prayers is the Book of Psalms.

The Psalms, often called the "Prayer Book" of the Bible, have provided comfort, hope, and strength for countless generations. Their enduring power lies not only in their poetic beauty, but also in their ability to capture the full range of human emotions. Whether in moments of joy, trust, and gratitude, or times of fear, sorrow, and doubt, the psalmists give voice to the deepest cries of the human soul. As the theologian Tremper Longman III suggests, the Psalms serve as a "mirror of the soul," reflecting our own emotional and spiritual experiences. Through their words, we can find language to express emotions that may otherwise be too complex or painful to articulate on our own.[7]

When we turn to the Psalms in prayer, we enter into a centuries-old tradition of honest and authentic communication with God. The psalmists held nothing back—whether they were praising God for deliverance, pleading for justice, or crying out in despair, they offered the fullness of their hearts to the One who listens. This transparency invites us to do the same. We don't need polished or perfect words to approach God. In fact, the Psalms remind us that prayer is not about performance but about relationship. It is the raw outpouring of the heart in whatever state we find ourselves—whether in joy, sorrow, anger, or hope.

Praying the Psalms gives us a way to engage with God when our own words fall short. These ancient prayers can become our prayers. For example, when we feel overwhelmed by life's burdens and cannot express the depth of our pain, we can turn to Psalm 130: "Out of the depths I cry to you, O Lord! O Lord, hear my voice!" In moments of deep gratitude, when we want to express thanks for God's presence, Psalm 103 can offer us language: "Bless the Lord, O my soul, and all that is within me, bless His holy name!" The Psalms cover every emotion and experience, offering us a way to stay connected to God through both the highs and lows of life.

Moreover, the Psalms are not only personal prayers; they also serve as communal prayers. Many of the Psalms were written in the plural, reflecting the collective voice of the people of Israel. Prayers like Psalm 80, "Restore us, O God; let your face shine, that we may be saved!", remind us that we are part of a larger community of faith. As we pray these Psalms, we join with believers from all times and places who have sought God's help, healing, and deliverance. This communal dimension of the Psalms is particularly

ROOTED IN DISCIPLESHIP

significant in times of societal crisis or when we feel isolated in our struggles. Praying these ancient words can remind us that we are never truly alone.

In praying the Psalms, we learn that there is no situation or emotion too small or too big to bring before God. From the heights of joy to the depths of despair, the psalmists teach us that God is present in every circumstance, and prayer is the pathway that leads us into a deeper relationship with the Divine. Even when our own words escape us, the Psalms provide a way forward, offering words that can carry us through difficult seasons and times of uncertainty.

Howard Thurman's insight into the complexities of life is a reminder that prayer, too, is complex—sometimes simple and spontaneous, sometimes structured and intentional. The Psalms invite us into both forms. While they provide a structured framework for prayer, they also give us the freedom to express our most personal thoughts and feelings. When we pray the Psalms, we don't just recite words; we enter into an ancient conversation with God, one that has been sustained across the ages and continues to shape the spiritual lives of millions today.

Praying the Scriptures, particularly the Psalms, becomes a way to integrate our faith into the daily realities of life. Whether we are seeking help, healing, deliverance, or simply longing to be in God's presence, the Psalms give us the language to do so. In moments when our own words fail, these ancient prayers become a lifeline, reminding us that we are held by a God who listens, understands, and journeys with us.

The list below offers categories to help you navigate through some of the Psalms:

1. Psalms of Praise and Worship (Psalms 8, 19, 29, 33, 100, 103, 145, 150)

Use these psalms to express worship and gratitude, focusing on God's greatness and His work in the world.

These psalms focus on adoration and exaltation of God's majesty, power, and glory. They often celebrate God's creation, goodness, and faithfulness.

2. Psalms of Thanksgiving (Psalms 30, 65, 66, 92, 107, 116, 136)

Pray with these psalms to give thanks for God's provision, guidance, and answered prayers in your life.

These psalms express gratitude for God's blessings and deliverance from difficult situations. They often recount specific moments when God has intervened to provide help or salvation.

PRAYERS

3. Psalms of Lament (Psalms 13, 22, 42, 69, 74, 77, 130)

Use these psalms when you are struggling, facing loss, or feeling distant from God. They help you express pain and trust in God's deliverance.

These psalms express sorrow, distress, or mourning. They often involve a cry for help in times of trouble, suffering, or injustice, while still affirming trust in God's care.

4. Psalms of Trust and Confidence (Psalms 23, 27, 46, 62, 91, 121, 125)

These psalms are useful when you want to affirm your faith in God's care and protection, even amidst adversity.

These psalms express a deep trust in God's protection, provision, and faithfulness even in difficult or uncertain times.

5. Psalms of Repentance (Psalms 32, 38, 51, 130, 143)

Use these psalms when seeking forgiveness, acknowledging sin, and asking for a renewed spirit.

These psalms are prayers of confession and repentance, asking for God's forgiveness and restoration after sin or wrongdoing.

6. Royal Psalms (Psalms 2, 18, 20, 45, 72, 110)

These psalms can be prayed in times of asking for godly leadership, protection over nations, and the fulfillment of God's promises.

These psalms focus on the role of the king, often celebrating God's covenant with David and His people. They may also refer prophetically to the coming Messiah.

4. Psalms of Wisdom (Psalms 1, 37, 49, 73, 112, 119)

Use these psalms when seeking guidance, wisdom, and understanding of God's ways in your life.

These psalms offer insights into how to live a life that pleases God, emphasizing the importance of following God's law and seeking His wisdom.

8. Imprecatory Psalms (Psalms 35, 58, 69, 83, 109, 137)

These psalms may be used when seeking justice and deliverance from evil, while also entrusting God with the outcome.

ROOTED IN DISCIPLESHIP

These psalms contain cries for justice and vengeance against enemies or oppressors. They are raw expressions of anger and a desire for God to intervene in situations of injustice.

9. Psalms of Remembrance and History (Psalms 78, 105, 106, 135, 136)

Use these psalms to remember and reflect on God's faithfulness throughout history and in your own life.

These psalms recount Israel's history and God's faithfulness through generations. They remind the people of God's acts of salvation, protection, and provision in the past.

Reflection on Praying the Psalms:

1. Complexity of Life and Prayer:

- ➢ Have you experienced moments in your life when you struggled to find the words to pray due to grief, anxiety, or confusion? How did that impact your connection with God?
- ➢ How does the notion that "God knows our needs before we speak" influence your understanding of prayer, especially when words feel insufficient?

2. Healing Through Expressing Emotions:

- ➢ Bringing our deepest emotions before God in prayer can be a path toward healing. Have you ever felt a sense of healing or relief after expressing your emotions to God through prayer?
- ➢ Which Psalm do you feel most drawn to during difficult times, and why do you think that particular Psalm resonates with you?

3. Honesty in Prayer:

- ➢ The psalmists approached God with honesty, expressing joy, despair, gratitude, or anger. How easy or difficult is it for you to bring your raw and honest emotions before God in prayer?
- ➢ How does knowing that prayer "is not about performance but about relationship" change the way you approach God in prayer?

4. Personalizing the Psalms:

- ➢ Psalm 130 says, *"Out of the depths I cry to you, O Lord! O Lord, hear my voice!"* Reflect on a time when you felt overwhelmed and turned

PRAYERS

to God. How might praying this Psalm have given you words when your own voice faltered?
- Psalm 103 begins with *"Bless the Lord, O my soul, and all that is within me, bless His holy name!"* How might this Psalm help you express gratitude when you feel God's presence in your life?

5. *Communal and Personal Prayer:*
- Many Psalms, such as Psalm 80, were written as communal prayers. How might praying these Psalms in a community or church setting help foster a sense of unity and shared faith?
- In times of personal struggle or societal crisis, how can praying the Psalms remind you that you are part of a larger community of faith that transcends time and space?

6. *God's Presence in Every Circumstance:*
- The psalmists teach us that God is present in every situation, whether it be joy or despair. Reflect on a time in your life when you felt God's presence during a difficult situation. How did prayer, or the lack of it, shape that experience?
- How do the Psalms help you stay connected to God, even when life feels overwhelming or uncertain?

7. *Navigating Different Types of Psalms:*
- The Psalms offer various categories such as praise, thanksgiving, lament, trust, and repentance. Is there a particular category that you find yourself turning to more frequently in your prayer life? Why do you think that is?
- How might praying the Psalms of Trust (such as Psalm 23 or Psalm 27) help you develop a deeper confidence in God's protection and faithfulness during times of adversity?

8. *Imprecatory Psalms and Seeking Justice:*
- Imprecatory Psalms, such as Psalm 35 or Psalm 137, express raw emotions like anger and a cry for justice. How do you feel about praying these types of Psalms? How can these Psalms guide you in bringing your desire for justice and vengeance before God?
- What does it mean to trust God with the outcome, even when praying for justice in the face of evil or oppression?

ROOTED IN DISCIPLESHIP

9. The Psalms as a Lifeline:
- ➤ How might praying the Psalms serve as a spiritual lifeline during seasons when you feel distant from God or when your own words escape you?
- ➤ Reflect on a time when you used scripture or a Psalm to pray. How did that shape your experience of prayer and your relationship with God?

10. Incorporating the Psalms into Daily Life:
- ➤ How can you incorporate the Psalms into your daily prayer practice, whether during times of need, thanksgiving, or reflection on God's faithfulness?
- ➤ Are there particular Psalms you feel called to explore more deeply? How might spending time with these Psalms enhance your spiritual life?

Types of Prayers

Prayer takes many forms, reflecting the diverse ways we communicate with God and express the concerns of our hearts.

Each type of prayer allows us to engage with God in a unique way, meeting the needs of different seasons of life and spiritual growth. Here are several primary types of prayer:

1. **Adoration (Praise):** This type of prayer focuses on the greatness and goodness of God. It's an opportunity to worship and honor God for who God is, not just for what God has done. Psalms like Psalm 8 and 145 are examples of prayers of adoration that glorify God's name and works.

2. **Confession:** Confessional prayers acknowledge our sins, shortcomings, and need for God's forgiveness. This type of prayer is essential for spiritual growth, as it leads to repentance and restoration with God. Psalm 51 is a model of a prayer of confession, where David seeks forgiveness after his sin with Bathsheba.

3. **Thanksgiving:** These prayers express gratitude for God's blessings, guidance, and provision. Through thanksgiving, we recognize that all good things come from God. Philippians 4:6 reminds us to pray with

PRAYERS

thanksgiving, while many of the Psalms, such as Psalm 100, express gratitude.

4. **Supplication (Petition):** This is the most common type of prayer, where we present our personal needs and desires to God. Philippians 4:6 encourages us to bring all our requests to God, knowing that God hears and answers prayers according to divine will.

5. **Intercession:** Intercessory prayers are those offered on behalf of others. We lift up friends, family, communities, and even the world in prayer, asking for God's intervention. Jesus himself modeled intercessory prayer in John 17 when he prayed for his disciples and for all believers.

6. **Meditation and Contemplation:** These types of prayers focus on silent reflection and being in God's presence. Rather than speaking, these prayers involve listening and resting in the stillness of God's Spirit. Contemplative prayer often includes a focus on Scripture or simply sitting in the awareness of God's presence.

7. **Lament:** Lament prayers are cries of sorrow, frustration, or grief. These prayers are often born out of suffering, where we seek God's comfort or intervention. Psalms of lament, like Psalm 22 or Psalm 13, show us how to pour out our deep pain to God while trusting in God's faithfulness.

Each of these types of prayers allows for a different kind of spiritual engagement. Whether through praise, repentance, supplication, or lament, we find ways to stay connected to God's presence and purposes in our lives.

Growing in Prayer

Prayer is a practice that evolves as we deepen our relationship with God. Just as relationships grow over time, our prayer life can develop from simple requests into more profound experiences of God's presence and guidance. Here are some practical steps and tips to help you grow in prayer:

1. **Consistency:** Like any spiritual discipline, consistency is key to growth in prayer. Set aside a specific time each day to pray. Whether it's first thing in the morning or before bed, having a set routine helps you develop a habit of prayer.

2. **Expand Your Methods:** Don't limit yourself to one type of prayer. Try different methods—silent prayer, journaling, praying Scripture,

or praying with others. Using different approaches can deepen your experience and make prayer more engaging.

3. **Incorporate Scripture:** The Bible can be a powerful guide for prayer. Use passages from Psalms, the Gospels, or epistles as prayers. Praying Scripture aligns your heart with God's Word and helps you pray according to God's will.

4. **Practice Listening:** Prayer is not just about speaking to God, but also about listening. Set aside moments of silence in your prayer time to simply listen for God's voice. This practice deepens your connection with God and opens you to divine guidance.

5. **Pray with Others:** Engaging in group prayer can strengthen your personal prayer life. Join a prayer group or meet with a prayer partner. The experience of praying together fosters community and allows for mutual encouragement.

6. **Use Written Prayers:** If you're unsure of what to say, written prayers can provide structure. The Lord's Prayer, prayers from the Book of Common Prayer, or hymns like those of Charles Wesley can be useful in guiding your thoughts and words during prayer.

7. **Focus on Presence Over Perfection:** Don't strive for the "perfect" prayer. God desires your presence, not perfection. Be authentic, open, and honest in your prayers. As your relationship with God grows, your prayers will naturally deepen.

8. **Cultivate a Heart of Gratitude:** Regularly give thanks for the ways God has answered prayers, even in small ways. Keeping a prayer journal where you record prayer requests and answers can remind you of God's faithfulness and inspire more consistent prayer.

Reflection Questions:

1. How do you typically communicate with God in prayer—through words, silence, or journaling?
2. Which type of prayer (adoration, confession, thanksgiving, supplication, etc.) do you feel most drawn to? Why?
3. In what ways could you expand or deepen your prayer life this week?
4. How do you think praying with others might help you grow in your relationship with God?

PRAYERS

5. Reflecting on your prayer journey, where have you seen God's faithfulness in answering prayers, and where do you still feel called to trust?

> **THE BELIEVERS DEVOTED THEMSELVES TO THE APOSTLES' TEACHING, TO THE COMMUNITY, TO THEIR SHARED MEALS, AND TO THEIR PRAYERS.**
>
> ACTS 2:42, CEB

PART 3
PRESENCE
Being Fully Present in Community

Introduction

Two disciples were walking a dusty road, heavy with grief. The one they had hoped would redeem Israel had been crucified. Their hearts were full of sorrow and confusion. As they talked and wrestled with what had happened, a stranger came alongside them. He didn't begin with a sermon or a solution. He simply joined them—listening, walking, and eventually, sharing a meal. It was only in the breaking of bread that their eyes were opened, and they recognized him: the risen Christ (Luke 24:13-35).

This is the ministry of presence. It's not flashy or loud. It often goes unnoticed until hearts begin to burn with the warmth of being seen, known, and loved. Presence is the decision to walk with others, especially when the right path is unclear. It is a sacred, incarnational practice that echoes the very heart of Christ.

The vow of presence is a profound expression of discipleship. It calls us to show up fully—physically, emotionally, and spiritually—for one another. More than just being in the room, presence is about being attentive, engaged, and open to the movement of God in shared life. As United Methodists, we

ROOTED IN DISCIPLESHIP

promise presence not merely as a form of attendance, but as an offering of ourselves to God and to the community of faith.

In our tradition, presence is a means of grace—a channel through which God's love flows to us and through us.[8] John Wesley emphasized the essential role of Christian fellowship in the life of faith.[9] For Wesley, presence was not merely a social activity, but a spiritual discipline that deepens our relationship with God and one another.[10] When we show up for others with attentiveness and compassion, we embody the grace that transforms hearts.

Presence does not require special skills or perfect words. Often, it means sitting in silence, listening without judgment, or simply staying close through seasons of struggle and celebration. Our very being—offered in love—is often more powerful than anything we can say or do. Through presence, we affirm the dignity and worth of others and reflect Christ's love in concrete ways.

Wesley understood this well. The Methodist movement was grounded in small groups—class meetings and bands—where believers "watched over one another in love."[11] These were spaces where presence was expected and treasured, where grace was encountered in honest conversation, shared burdens, and mutual support. Wesley knew that discipleship could not happen in isolation. It required people showing up for one another, again and again.

Jesus modeled this ministry throughout His life. He dined with sinners, touched the sick, and wept with the grieving. He did not remain distant or removed. He entered into the fullness of our humanity. In His presence, people found healing, hope, and belonging. When we walk with others as He did, we continue His incarnational mission in the world.

Presence also builds a community where transformation can occur.[12] When we commit to being present with and for one another, we create a space where spiritual growth takes root. In such communities, accountability, encouragement, and grace flourish. Wesley believed that ongoing presence—faithfully showing up—was necessary for real change to happen in our hearts and lives.

Finally, presence begins with attentiveness to God. As we cultivate awareness of God's nearness, we are better able to be present with others. We become vessels of peace, hope, and healing—channels through which God's Spirit moves. In a culture often marked by distraction and disconnection, the ministry of presence is a countercultural act of love and faith.

The vow of presence is not about perfect attendance. It is about faithful availability—to God and to one another. It is a living witness to the truth that

PRESENCE

we are not alone. Just as Christ walked the Emmaus road with two confused disciples, He now invites us to do the same for others: to walk with them, listen to them, and break bread together in holy love.

Examples of Practicing the Ministry of Presence

The ministry of presence can be expressed in various ways throughout the life of the church and in our daily interactions, making a tangible impact on individuals and the wider community. Here are some examples that reflect how this ministry can be practiced:

1. **Worship Attendance:** Being consistently present in worship services is one of the most straightforward yet profound ways to practice the ministry of presence. When we gather for worship, we not only nurture our own spirits but also encourage those around us. Our presence in worship signifies that we value communal gatherings and see them as essential to our spiritual lives. Together, we hear God's Word, share in the sacraments, and offer praise as one body in Christ, reminding one another that we belong to a faith community that values shared experiences.

2. **Small Group Participation:** Small groups, Bible studies, and discipleship classes are opportunities to grow deeper in faith while supporting others in their journey. Within these gatherings, we can actively listen, share our perspectives, and hold one another accountable. Small groups provide a setting where vulnerability is welcomed, and personal growth is nurtured, allowing us to experience God's grace through the authentic sharing of our lives.

3. **Being Present for Those in Crisis:** Offering our presence to someone who is experiencing hardship—whether due to illness, loss, or emotional distress—embodies Christ's love in a deeply compassionate way. This might involve visiting someone in the hospital, sitting with someone in their grief, or checking in on someone who feels isolated. In these moments, words are often secondary to simply being there, allowing the person to feel seen, heard, and valued.

4. **Community Events and Outreach:** Attending or supporting church-sponsored events and community outreach activities provides an opportunity to extend the ministry of presence beyond the church walls. When we show up for these events, we become visible ambassadors of

our faith, building connections within the community and representing a church that cares for its neighbors.

5. **Celebrating Life's Milestones:** The ministry of presence also involves celebrating moments of joy, such as birthdays, graduations, and anniversaries. Showing up for one another during life's milestones strengthens the bonds within the church community, affirming that we rejoice with each other in times of joy just as we support each other in times of sorrow.

6. **Intentional Listening and Support:** Sometimes, the most meaningful gift we can offer is a listening ear. Taking the time to ask someone how they're really doing and then listening with empathy allows people to feel valued. Whether it's over a coffee or during a pastoral visit, intentional listening creates a sacred space where people can open their hearts, share their struggles, and find encouragement.

Reflection Questions:

Reflecting on the ministry of presence can deepen our understanding of how we embody this commitment. Consider the following questions:

- ➢ When you attend worship or other church gatherings, how do you prepare yourself to be fully present?
- ➢ Are there areas in your life where you feel called to be more present for others? What might that look like?
- ➢ Think of a time when someone offered you the gift of their presence. How did it impact you, and what did you learn from the experience?
- ➢ How can you cultivate attentiveness to both God's presence and the needs of those around you?
- ➢ In what ways can you practice the ministry of presence within your family, workplace, and church community?
- ➢ How does being present with others help you grow in your relationship with God?

What is Worship?

Worship is an intentional act of acknowledging God's worth and glory, rooted in relationship and shaped by grace. It is our response to the self-giving love of God—a posture of reverence, gratitude, and devotion. At its core, worship

PRESENCE

is the act of ascribing worth to God, aligning our whole selves—body, mind, and spirit—toward the One who is Creator, Sustainer, and Redeemer of all. The word *worship* comes from the Old English *weorthscipe*, meaning "to give worth to," and this etymology reminds us that worship begins not with ourselves, but with the recognition of God's majesty and mercy.

In the Wesleyan tradition, worship is not only individual but deeply communal. It is a shared discipline in which the gathered body of believers is shaped by God's presence and drawn into the life of Christ. Worship is a means of grace—a channel through which God forms and transforms us. Through prayer, the reading of Scripture, the celebration of sacraments, and the singing of hymns, God's Spirit actively works in us to renew our hearts and align our lives with divine purposes.[13] This grace does not merely comfort—it reshapes, challenges, and sanctifies.

Worship is inherently relational and dialogic.[14] It is not a one-sided offering or a static ritual but a living conversation between God and the people of God. The divine initiative comes first, calling us into communion, and we respond with praise, confession, intercession, and thanksgiving. In this sacred rhythm of call and response, God speaks and we answer—not only with words, but with our lives. Worship immerses us in the story of salvation and reorients us to our true identity and vocation in Christ.

Within this framework, worship is not confined to one hour on a Sunday. It is a way of life that continues beyond the sanctuary, shaping every aspect of our daily living. When worship is rightly practiced, it forms us into a people of compassion and justice.[15] Our adoration becomes action. Love for God spills over into love for neighbor. This holistic vision of worship insists that devotion to God must manifest in a life of integrity, service, and mercy. The whole of life becomes liturgy—an offering that reflects God's love to the world.

Sacramental practices such as Baptism and Holy Communion further deepen the formative power of worship. These sacred actions are not merely symbolic but are means of grace through which we encounter the real presence of Christ.[16] In the waters of baptism, we are named, claimed, and initiated into the covenant community. At the Table, we receive the nourishment of Christ's body and blood, drawing strength for the journey of discipleship. In both, the Holy Spirit moves in mysterious and transformative ways, binding us to one another and renewing us for mission.

Worship, then, is a dynamic and holistic practice. It draws us into the mystery of God, forms us in the image of Christ, and equips us to live as faithful

ROOTED IN DISCIPLESHIP

witnesses in the world. In the Wesleyan tradition, worship is not simply something we attend—it is something that attends to us. It is where heaven touches earth, and where God's grace meets us again and again, shaping a people who reflect divine love in word, deed, and community.

Reflection Questions

1. The Meaning and Essence of Worship

- How might understanding worship as acknowledging God's worth affect your approach to worship?
- The term "weorthscipe" suggests honoring God's worth through intentional alignment of body, mind, and spirit. How do you see this alignment in your own worship practices? Are there areas where you feel more or less connected?
- Reflecting on the relational aspect of worship, what aspects of your relationship with God feel most emphasized in worship for you (e.g., reverence, gratitude, devotion)? How might you bring those aspects more fully into your daily life?

2. Worship as a Means of Grace and Transformation

- When has worship been a transformative experience for you? What about that experience felt impactful?
- Worship engages both individual and communal elements. How does worship in community enhance your individual faith journey? What benefits or challenges does communal worship bring to your personal experience of God's grace?
- How do you think about worship as part of a lifestyle? What are ways you can intentionally incorporate worship into your daily routines?

3. Worship as a Dialogic Encounter

- Worship is described as a "dialogic encounter" where we engage in a divine conversation. In what ways do you feel that God "speaks" to you in worship? How do you typically respond to this communication?
- Consider the idea that worship invites us into the larger narrative of God's work in the world. How do you see your personal story fitting into this greater story of faith? How does worship help you to better understand your role in God's creation?

4. Worship, Sacraments, and Symbols

- ➢ Sacraments are central to Christian worship and offer a tangible experience of God's grace. How do you experience God's presence in the sacraments of Communion and Baptism? What does participation in these sacraments mean to you personally?
- ➢ What symbols or rituals hold particular meaning for you in worship? How do they help you connect with the larger story of God's salvation?

5. Worship as a Way of Life

- ➢ Wesley believed that worship extends beyond ritual to a way of life that includes service, justice, and love for God and neighbor. How does this view challenge or affirm your current understanding of worship?
- ➢ Reflecting on Wesley's idea that every action can be worshipful, consider aspects of your daily life—work, relationships, service—where you might see opportunities to worship God. How can you make these moments more intentional acts of worship?

6. Reflection on Community and Worship's Purpose

- ➢ In what ways does communal worship strengthen your connection to God and to others? How does the community of believers help you grow in grace and deepen your relationship with God?
- ➢ Worship is an act of aligning with God's purposes. Are there specific practices or spiritual disciplines that you feel called to develop as you seek to align fully with God in worship?

Why Do We Worship?

We worship because of who God is and what God has done. Worship is our faithful response to the grace of God, a holy act of gratitude and reverence toward the One who creates, redeems, and sustains all things. It is not merely a religious obligation but a joyful answer to God's invitation into covenant relationship. Through worship, we taste the fullness of life found in communion with the living God.

From the earliest biblical traditions, worship has included the offering of gifts to God. In ancient Israel, sacrifices and symbolic rituals expressed gratitude, repentance, and dependence. Today, though the form has changed, the spirit of offering remains. Our worship becomes a spiritual sacrifice—our time, our

ROOTED IN DISCIPLESHIP

attention, our prayers, our presence—all offered to God in love. Worship is a means of grace: it is the space where we receive God's renewing presence, and it is also the act through which we offer ourselves to be shaped by divine love.[17]

Worship nurtures and sustains the soul. In a world of distraction and weariness, worship grounds us in God's love and renews our sense of purpose. It protects us against spiritual apathy and anchors us in the truth of God's faithfulness. Through Scripture, prayer, and especially the sacraments, we are reminded of God's promises and drawn into deeper intimacy with the Spirit. Holy Communion in particular becomes both nourishment and commissioning. As we share in the bread and cup, we remember Christ's sacrifice and receive the grace to live as his body in the world.[18]

Worship is also essential to Christian community. The early church understood this deeply. As Acts 2:42 describes, the first believers devoted themselves to teaching, fellowship, the breaking of bread, and prayer—worship as the heartbeat of their shared life. This pattern continues in the church today. Worship binds us together as members of Christ's body. It reminds us that we are not alone; we belong to a people who have sought God's presence across generations and around the world. In gathering to worship, we are formed in mutual love and accountability.

Furthermore, worship is a public witness. It proclaims to the world that God is worthy, and that we belong to a different kind of kingdom—one marked by mercy, justice, and love. In Wesleyan theology, worship is inseparable from the call to social holiness. The experience of God's presence in worship must overflow into lives of compassion and service. Worship that remains confined within the sanctuary is incomplete. When we rise from prayer and praise, we are sent out to be Christ's hands and feet in the world, to seek justice, lift the lowly, and bear witness to the transforming power of grace.[19]

In sum, we worship to draw nearer to God, to nourish our souls, to live more fully in community, and to bear witness to the good news of Jesus Christ. Worship is not just something we do—it is something God uses to shape who we are. In worship, we are transformed from the inside out, equipped to reflect God's love in all that we do. It is here that we find strength for the journey, renewed by grace and empowered to live as faithful disciples.

PRESENCE

Reflection Questions:

1. Recognizing God's Nature and Actions
- When you think about who God is and what God has done, what aspect of God's nature do you feel most drawn to in worship?
- How does viewing worship as a response rather than a duty affect your desire to worship?
- What acts of worship (prayer, song, Communion) help you experience God's grace and presence most deeply? Why do you think these resonate with you?

2. Worship as Offering and Connection
- How do you understand the concept of worship as an offering to God? What are some ways you can offer yourself in worship beyond the church setting?
- Worship is often called a "means of grace" that channels God's love and strength. In what ways has worship strengthened or encouraged you in your faith journey?
- What practices or attitudes help you feel connected to God during worship? Are there any distractions or obstacles that you struggle with?

3. Spiritual Sustenance and Communion
- Worship is said to "nurture the soul" and guard against spiritual complacency. How has worship been a source of strength or renewal for you in challenging times?
- Communion reminds us of Christ's sacrifice and calls us to service. How does participating in Communion shape your understanding of worship as both a gift received and a call to action?
- Reflect on how worship unites us as a community. How does worshiping with others deepen your experience of faith?

4. Worship as Community and Witness
- Worship was central to the life of the early church, as seen in Acts 2:42. How does communal worship help you feel connected to the larger story of the church?
- How does worship inspire you to live out your faith in service to others? Are there ways worship encourages you to reach out to those who are marginalized or in need?

ROOTED IN DISCIPLESHIP

> ➤ In what ways does worship help you recognize your part in the broader Christian community across time and place?

5. *Worship as Transformation and Call to Action*
> ➤ John Wesley emphasized that worship should move us toward social holiness. How does worship inspire you to seek justice and mercy in your daily life?
> ➤ How do you see worship as a preparation for living out your faith in the world? What specific actions or commitments does worship call you to embody?
> ➤ Worship is described as a means by which we are transformed, "empowered to live as Christ's followers." How has worship shaped your understanding of discipleship or strengthened your walk with Christ?

Being Present in Worship

Worship stands at the heart of Christian discipleship. It is a sacred gathering where the body of Christ comes together to encounter God, hear the Word proclaimed, and participate in the sacraments that sustain our spiritual life. Far from being a routine event, worship is a transformative experience that reorients our hearts, renews our spirits, and strengthens our resolve to live as faithful disciples. Through this communal act, we open ourselves to the presence of the Holy Spirit and are drawn more deeply into the life and mission of God.

Being present in worship requires more than occupying a pew; it invites our full engagement—heart, mind, and spirit. This presence takes shape in our voices raised in song, our shared prayers, our listening to Scripture, and our mutual encouragement in the faith.

Worship participation reflects our love for God and our commitment to one another as members of Christ's body. The early church modeled this holistic participation, gathering regularly to learn, pray, and break bread together (Acts 2:42). For them, worship was not optional—it was essential to their identity and growth. So it is with us. To be present in worship is to take seriously our calling to grow in grace and community.

In the Wesleyan tradition, worship is considered a means of grace—a primary way in which God meets us and transforms us. John Wesley understood that worship was not simply edifying for individuals but vital for the building up of the whole community. He urged Methodists to gather often, believing that

PRESENCE

communal worship created the environment where the Spirit's sanctifying work could flourish.[20] It was in these gatherings that believers experienced conviction, consolation, and calling—evidence of God's grace at work among them.

Showing up for worship is both a spiritual discipline and an act of solidarity. It is a way of saying, "I belong here. I am part of what God is doing in this place." Regular attendance weaves a rhythm of grace into our lives, anchoring us through seasons of joy and sorrow. The habits of worship—prayer, Scripture, sacrament—become the scaffolding for a life formed by Christ. It is in the act of showing up that we are shaped by God's love and empowered for service in the world.

Being present in worship also strengthens our relationships within the church. The gathered community reminds us that faith is never meant to be a solitary journey. We are called to bear one another's burdens, to rejoice and to grieve together, to be held accountable in love (Galatians 6:2). Worship connects us to a larger story—a communion of saints across time and space—and helps us see our lives as part of God's unfolding mission.[21]

This gathering is not simply for our benefit; it is also a witness to the world. The simple act of coming together to worship testifies to the reality of God's love and the hope of Christ. Wesley believed that true worship must lead to holy living—that the grace we receive in worship should shape our daily lives.[22] When we prioritize being present in worship, we embody the vows we have made: to uphold the church through our prayers, our presence, our gifts, our service, and our witness.

Every Sunday becomes a moment of reorientation. In worship, we encounter God's mercy anew, are reminded of our belovedness, and are commissioned once more to be Christ's presence in the world. This regular rhythm forms us slowly and deeply, teaching us how to pray, how to forgive, how to hope, and how to live.

To be present in worship, then, is to participate in God's transforming grace. It is a discipline that deepens our love for God and one another, a communal act that strengthens our faith, and a visible sign of our commitment to the life of discipleship. When we gather as the body of Christ, we experience the renewing power of God's Spirit—and through that presence, we are made ready to love and serve in Christ's name.

ROOTED IN DISCIPLESHIP

Discussion Questions

- What does "being present" in worship mean to you? How does it differ from simply attending a service?
- Reflect on a time when attending worship strengthened or renewed your faith. How did the experience impact you?
- How does gathering for worship connect us to the early church's practices, as described in Acts 2:42?
- In what ways does regular worship attendance help deepen your relationship with God and strengthen your commitment to the faith community?
- How might worship attendance serve as a form of witness to others, both inside and outside the church?
- Wesley believed communal worship to be a means of grace. How does thinking of worship attendance in this way influence your view of its importance?
- What steps can you take to be more engaged and present during worship services?

The Ways We Worship

The ways in which we worship are as varied as the body of Christ itself, shaped by tradition, culture, and context. In the Wesleyan tradition, worship is a holistic and embodied response to God's grace—an active participation in the means through which God shapes and sanctifies us. Whether through prayer, proclamation, sacrament, song, or giving, each element of worship invites us into deeper communion with God and with one another.

- **Prayer:** Prayer is foundational to worship. It is the language of relationship, opening a sacred space for communion between Creator and creation. In the Wesleyan understanding, prayer is not only personal but communal—a practice that forms us in humility, gratitude, dependence, and hope. To "pray without ceasing" (1 Thessalonians 5:17, ESV) is to cultivate a life attentive to God's presence. In worship, we offer prayers of adoration, confession, thanksgiving, and intercession, lifting our voices together in trust that God hears and responds.[23] Through prayer, we bring our whole selves before God, allowing grace to meet us in our vulnerability and transform our hearts.

PRESENCE

- **Scripture and Sermon:** The reading and proclamation of Scripture hold a central place in Christian worship. Scripture is the primary means by which we hear God's voice, and the sermon becomes a moment of holy interpretation, where the Word is opened and applied to our lives. Wesley believed that the faithful preaching of Scripture has the power to convict of sin, awaken faith, offer comfort, and stir us toward holiness.[24] Preaching is not mere instruction—it is proclamation that calls us to embody the gospel in our thoughts, words, and actions. It invites us to hear anew the story of God's redeeming love and to take our place within it.

- **Sacraments:** Baptism and Holy Communion are the sacred signs through which God's grace is conveyed in visible and tangible form. Wesley taught that the sacraments are not empty rituals, but living encounters with Christ. Baptism marks our welcome into the family of God, initiating us into the life of discipleship and signifying the gift of new life. Communion is the ongoing feast that nourishes and sustains us, a meal where Christ is truly present to forgive, strengthen, and send us out in love. These holy mysteries serve as reminders that God's grace is not abstract but embodied—offered to us again and again through water, bread, and cup.[25]

- **Music and Singing:** Music is a sacred gift that allows us to worship with the fullness of emotion, intellect, and spirit. In the Wesleyan tradition, singing is more than embellishment—it is theological formation and communal prayer. Charles Wesley's hymns are a testament to the power of music to shape belief and stir the soul. When we sing together, we are united in praise, lament, hope, and thanksgiving. Music enables us to respond to God with our whole selves, lifting our hearts and voices in joyful worship that transcends spoken word.

- **Offering:** The offering is both a practical and spiritual act—a moment when we present a portion of our lives back to God. It is a response to God's generosity and a recognition that all we have belongs to God. To give is to participate in the mission of the church and to express our desire to be stewards of grace. Our financial offerings support ministry, service, and the extension of God's justice in the world. But more than that, they symbolize the deeper offering of our lives, as we seek to live generously and selflessly for the sake of others.[26]

ROOTED IN DISCIPLESHIP

These practices are not isolated rituals but interwoven expressions of faith. Together, they form a liturgy that engages our bodies, minds, and spirits—drawing us more fully into the transforming presence of God. In the Wesleyan tradition, worship is not a passive event but an active, grace-filled encounter that shapes us for holy living. It is here that we are reminded of God's ongoing work in the world and are invited to participate in that work, embodying Christ's love, justice, and mercy in all we do.

Reflection Questions:

- How might you integrate a more prayerful attitude into your everyday life?
- How does hearing scripture read and explained in worship differ from reading it on your own? What impact does this shared experience have on your faith?
- How do you experience God's grace through the sacraments during worship?
- Reflect on a hymn or worship song that has resonated deeply with you. How does music help you express your faith in a way words alone cannot?
- How does the perspective that our resources are entrusted to us by God to serve others shape your view of the offering as part of worship?
- In what ways has worship transformed you for a life of love, service, or justice?
- As you consider your own worship practices, where do you sense God calling you to grow or deepen your response to God's grace?
- How can you embody Christ's presence in your daily life as an extension of your worship?

Small Groups and Fellowship

In addition to corporate worship, the ministry of presence extends into Sunday School, small groups, Bible studies, and fellowship gatherings. These more intimate settings offer sacred space for deeper connection, encouragement, and spiritual formation. Discipleship is a lifelong journey, and these gatherings create the conditions for honest conversation, mutual accountability, and a shared pursuit of Christlikeness. Whether gathered around Scripture, united in prayer, or sharing a meal, these moments become spiritually nourishing as they invite us to grow in grace alongside others.

By participating in these smaller group settings, we offer more than our time—we offer ourselves. We demonstrate the value we place on community and affirm our shared calling to journey together in faith. In these spaces, we learn to "bear one another's burdens" (Galatians 6:2), creating a community that reflects the compassion and support of Christ. The vulnerability and attentiveness fostered in these gatherings allow God to work not only in us but through us, building up the body of Christ in profound and transformative ways.[27]

John Wesley believed that Christian fellowship was essential for growth in holiness. He established class meetings and bands as means of grace, where Methodists would gather weekly to "watch over one another in love" and to hold one another accountable in the life of faith.[28] These small groups were not merely social gatherings but instruments of spiritual awakening, discipleship, and communal support. Wesley understood that transformation does not happen in isolation—it occurs in the context of trusting, prayerful relationships.

Discipleship flourishes when nurtured by supportive relationships and shared practices of faith. As followers of Jesus Christ, we are called to deepen our love for God and neighbor through active involvement in community life. Small groups are a vital expression of this calling. They foster spiritual growth, offer space for mutual care, and help connect personal faith with communal mission. Through shared prayer, reflection on Scripture, and acts of service, small groups equip disciples to live out the vows of prayer, presence, gifts, service, and witness with greater intention and joy.

Ultimately, the work of small groups is to shape hearts for love—love of God, love of neighbor, and love that moves toward mission. These gatherings cultivate lives rooted in grace and committed to transformation, forming a people who are being shaped not only for spiritual growth, but also for compassionate action in the world.

Why Small Groups

As we have explored, discipleship is an intentional process of spiritual formation. While the shape of this journey may change throughout different seasons of life, certain truths remain consistent: we are formed most fully in community, and spiritual growth flourishes when nurtured in accountable, grace-filled relationships. Small groups provide the intentional space needed to cultivate that kind of transformation.

ROOTED IN DISCIPLESHIP

Small Groups Create Intentional Spaces for Connection and Growth:

Rooted in the Wesleyan tradition of class meetings and bands, small groups typically bring together 6–12 individuals who meet regularly to study Scripture, pray, and engage in acts of service. These gatherings foster authentic relationships and provide a safe, structured environment for participants to explore faith and deepen their walk with Christ.[29]

Small Groups Move Disciples Toward Active Engagement:

Discipleship is not passive. Small group participation invites individuals to move beyond mere attendance into active, life-changing engagement with God and neighbor. As members gather to share life and grow in grace, they begin to embody their faith in tangible ways—both within and beyond the church.

Cultivate Spiritual Growth and Accountability:

Small groups nurture spiritual maturity through rhythms of prayer, study, and mutual accountability. Participants are encouraged to take responsibility for their own spiritual journey while walking alongside others. This pattern reflects John Wesley's belief that grace is mediated in community, and that we grow in love by watching over one another in love.[30]

Develop Leaders:

Small groups also serve as seedbeds for leadership development. By offering opportunities to lead prayer, facilitate discussion, or organize service projects, small groups equip members to exercise spiritual gifts and take on greater roles within the church and community. In doing so, they continue Wesley's vision of equipping laity for ministry and mission.

Types of Small Groups

Small groups take many forms to meet the needs of people in diverse life stages and spiritual journeys. Though varied in structure, they are unified by their commitment to foster growth in love of God and neighbor.
- ➢ **Covenant Groups:** Members commit to shared expectations around attendance, participation, and mutual accountability.
- ➢ **Affinity Groups:** These groups bring together individuals with similar interests or demographics (e.g., young adults, parents, men's and women's groups) to create supportive contexts for faith development.

PRESENCE

> **Open and Closed Groups:** Open groups welcome new participants at any time, while closed groups journey together for a defined period, building deeper trust and intimacy.

> **Support Groups:** Rooted in care and compassion, these groups address specific challenges—such as grief, addiction, or divorce—offering a faith-based community for healing and growth.

No matter the format, each group shares a common purpose: to help members grow as disciples by cultivating spiritual depth, relational integrity, and missional engagement.

Living into Our Discipleship Vows in Small Groups

Small groups provide a unique space to embody the vows of prayers, presence, gifts, service, and witness. These five commitments—central to life in The United Methodist Church—take on flesh in the context of deepening relationships and shared practices.

> **Prayers:** Groups gather regularly to lift one another in prayer, deepening intimacy with God and nurturing trust among members.

> **Presence:** Being present in a group means more than attending—it means showing up with vulnerability, attentiveness, and compassion.

> **Gifts:** Each participant brings unique spiritual gifts, talents, and perspectives that enrich the group and further the church's mission.

> **Service:** Groups often engage in mission together, reflecting Christ's love through concrete acts of mercy and justice in the community.

> **Witness:** Through storytelling, encouragement, and shared testimony, members practice articulating their faith and bearing witness to God's grace.[31]

Structure and Leadership of Small Groups

Small groups function best with flexible structure and spiritually grounded leadership. Leaders serve as facilitators, not instructors—guiding discussions, fostering inclusion, and modeling Christlike humility. Group leaders partner with participants to determine areas of study, service opportunities, and rhythms of meeting. They are supported by pastoral staff through ongoing training, prayer, and resource sharing. This collaborative leadership reflects the early Methodist vision of equipping the laity to lead spiritual communities marked by grace and accountability.[32]

ROOTED IN DISCIPLESHIP

Practical Examples of Living Out the Ministry of Presence in Small Groups

- ➢ **Commitment to Worship Together:** Small groups may attend worship services together, reinforcing the connection between small group life and the broader body of Christ.
- ➢ **Serving in Mission:** By organizing service projects such as food drives or shelter volunteering, groups embody the love of Christ through shared action.
- ➢ **Sharing Life's Joys and Struggles:** Whether celebrating a birth or walking through grief, small groups provide the relational support that reflects Christ's care.
- ➢ **Supporting Life Transitions:** In seasons of change—new jobs, illness, marriage, or loss—groups come alongside one another with prayer, presence, and practical help.

These expressions of presence reflect the early church's pattern of mutual care and the Wesleyan commitment to communal sanctification. Through small groups, discipleship becomes not only personal but relational, not only inward but outward—a movement of grace unfolding in everyday life.

Reflection Questions:

- ➢ In what ways does gathering in a small group deepen your experience of worship and discipleship?
- ➢ How do the different aspects of our discipleship vows—prayers, presence, gifts, service, and witness—manifest in your participation in a small group?
- ➢ How has sharing joys and struggles with others in a small group helped you understand the ministry of presence fully?
- ➢ How does participating in a small group support your ability to live out your faith in everyday life?
- ➢ How can your small group enhance its commitment to mutual support, accountability, and service in ways that extend beyond your regular meetings?

Showing Up for One Another

The ministry of presence extends beyond scheduled gatherings like worship and small groups. At its heart, presence is a spiritual practice of showing up—especially in times of need—with love, compassion, and attentiveness.

PRESENCE

Whether by visiting someone who is ill, offering a listening ear, or simply being there through seasons of grief or uncertainty, we live out our discipleship through this embodied form of care. Presence is more than physical proximity; it is an offering of emotional and spiritual support that reminds others they are not alone.

To be present with someone in suffering, celebration, or ordinary life is an act of love and solidarity. It affirms our belief that we are members of one body, interconnected by grace, and responsible for bearing one another's burdens. This is the kind of presence Christ modeled in his earthly ministry—attentive, compassionate, interruptible. When we choose to show up for each other, not out of obligation but out of love, we make space for the Spirit to work through us in quiet, powerful ways.[33]

The gift of presence does not require eloquent words or perfect solutions. It simply requires our attentiveness. To sit beside someone in silence, to hold their hand in grief, or to laugh with them in joy—these are holy acts. As we enter another's story with humility and care, we reflect Christ's love and affirm the sacred worth of those around us. In doing so, we bear witness not only to their value but also to the truth that God is already present with them.

This is the mystery of Christian presence: we do not bring Christ into another's experience—Christ is already there. Instead, we join in what God is already doing, bearing witness to God's nearness and grace.[34] This understanding deepens our faith and our connection to one another. In every encounter, we encounter Christ. In every moment of presence, we practice the gospel.

The Spiritual Practice of Presence

To be truly present is a spiritual discipline. It asks more of us than simply showing up in body. It requires attentiveness to the moment, to the other person, and to the presence of God.

In a world that often prizes distraction and busyness, presence calls us to slow down, to be still, and to notice. It invites us to center ourselves in prayer and to engage with our surroundings, our relationships, and our calling with intentionality.

This kind of presence is formed by grace. It is cultivated through practices that open our hearts to God—prayer, silence, scripture, and service. In learning to be present, we learn to see others as Christ sees them and to make room for love in our lives and schedules.

ROOTED IN DISCIPLESHIP

As Wesleyans, we understand that grace is not only something we receive but something we offer. Presence is one way we become vessels of that grace in the world.[35]

Whether in worship, in small group conversation, or while sitting at a hospital bedside, presence is a sacred act. It fosters trust, deepens community, and reflects the self-giving love of Christ. When we engage with our whole selves—heart, mind, body, and spirit—we create the kind of relationships that sustain faith and embody God's kingdom.

In this way, presence becomes a quiet but powerful form of ministry. It is discipleship made visible. It is love incarnate.

Reflection Questions:

- ➤ When you think about being present in worship or church gatherings, what emotions or thoughts arise? What draws you closer, or what might be holding you back?
- ➤ How has showing up for others in their times of need changed your understanding of Christian community?
- ➤ When have you experienced the gift of someone's presence in your life? How did that impact you, and what did it reveal about the power of presence?
- ➤ How might God be inviting you to be fully present in your church and community life?
- ➤ What intentional steps can you take to embody this vow of presence in the coming weeks?

> WE HAVE DIFFERENT GIFTS THAT ARE CONSISTENT WITH GOD'S GRACE THAT HAS BEEN GIVEN TO US. IF YOUR GIFT IS PROPHECY, YOU SHOULD PROPHESY IN PROPORTION TO YOUR FAITH. IF YOUR GIFT IS SERVICE, DEVOTE YOURSELF TO SERVING. IF YOUR GIFT IS TEACHING, DEVOTE YOURSELF TO TEACHING. IF YOUR GIFT IS ENCOURAGEMENT, DEVOTE YOURSELF TO ENCOURAGING. THE ONE GIVING SHOULD DO IT WITH NO STRINGS ATTACHED. THE LEADER SHOULD LEAD WITH PASSION. THE ONE SHOWING MERCY SHOULD BE CHEERFUL.
>
> ―― ROMANS 12:6-8 (CEB)

PART 4
GIFTS
Generosity as an Act of Worship

Introduction

The vow of gifts acknowledges that everything we have—our resources, time, talents, and passions—is a divine blessing entrusted to us for the good of others. In his letter to the Romans, Paul affirms the diversity of these gifts and their essential purpose in building up the body of Christ. Each gift, whether spiritual or practical, is a unique expression of God's grace working through us—not only for personal fulfillment, but to foster compassion, justice, worship, and community.

To vow our gifts is to commit to a life of gratitude and intentionality. We respond to God's generous grace by using what we have for God's purposes. This vow is not merely about charitable giving; it is central to the life of Christian discipleship, rooted in the belief that we are stewards—not owners—of all that we possess.

In the Wesleyan tradition, stewardship is both an inward journey of personal transformation and an outward expression of love and service. John Wesley taught that a life transformed by grace must bear visible fruit, including the

ROOTED IN DISCIPLESHIP

wise and generous use of one's gifts. "When the Possessor of heaven and earth brought you into being," Wesley preached, "and placed you in this world, he placed you here not as a proprietor, but as a steward."[36]

Thus, when we speak of "gifts," we are referring to every aspect of life that can be offered to God's mission. These include not only financial resources, but also spiritual gifts, natural talents, and the time we devote to serving others. Wesley encouraged early Methodists to view their whole selves—their head, hands, and heart—as tools for holy living and mission. "Employ whatever God has entrusted you with," he wrote, "in doing good, all possible good, in every possible kind and degree… Render unto God, not a tenth, not a third, not half, but all that is God's."[37]

This perspective reshapes our understanding of stewardship: our lives are not our own. Everything we have is a gift, and we are accountable to God for how we use it. Faithful discipleship calls us to align our use of gifts with God's mission of love, justice, and transformation in the world.

When we adopt a holistic view of stewardship, we begin to see our whole lives—our finances, skills, time, and passions—as ways to grow in grace and serve others. The Christian life becomes a disciplined, intentional journey grounded in prayer, accountability, and service, and marked by a deep commitment to offer our gifts in service to Christ.

The Apostle Paul reminds us again in Romans 12 that although our gifts are diverse, we are "one body in Christ, and individually we belong to each other" (Romans 12:5b, CEB). These gifts are not for private benefit but for the strengthening of the whole community.

While the variety of gifts is vast, we can group them into three primary dimensions that shape our spiritual development and practice of generosity:

Financial Gifts: Giving financially is a tangible expression of our trust in God and our investment in God's kingdom. Our generosity enables the church to fulfill its mission, support its ministries, and meet the needs of the community. In many congregations, intentional giving is encouraged not just as a duty but as an act of worship and faithfulness.

Spiritual Gifts: Beyond finances, we are called to offer our spiritual gifts—such as teaching, leadership, hospitality, music, administration, and more—for the work of the church.

Discipleship ministries help individuals discover and develop their spiritual gifts through formation opportunities, service projects, and leadership development.

Time and Talents: Offering our time and talents is another way we live out the vow of gifts. Whether volunteering at a church event, leading a small group, visiting the homebound, or going on a mission trip, each of us has something valuable to contribute to the community and to God's work in the world.

The vow of gifts challenges us to go beyond thinking about money alone.

It invites us to live with open hands and hearts, recognizing that the fullness of our lives is meant to be poured out in service, so that others might come to experience the great love of God through us.

A faithful discipleship system helps identify and activate these gifts, ensuring that everyone—no matter their age, income, or ability—has a meaningful role in the work of God's kingdom.

Reflection Questions:

- What do you envision when you consider the unique gifts God has entrusted to you?
- How do you feel called to use them, and where might there be uncertainty or excitement?
- When you think about giving financially or of your time, what inner movement do you notice?
- How might God be inviting you to trust Him in new ways through your generosity?
- As you reflect on your talents, where do you feel most alive in your service to others?
- How might God be calling you to explore new ways of offering your gifts?

Money Matters

In the Christian faith, money is often viewed as both a tool and a test. Jesus spoke about money frequently—not because he viewed it as an inherent evil or as a means to achieve holiness, but because how we handle money reflects our relationship with God and our values. Far from being a secular concern, money is deeply tied to our spiritual lives, shaping our interactions, priorities, and the ways we demonstrate our trust in God. Jesus understood that our financial practices reveal where our true commitments lie, as he told his followers, "For where your treasure is, there your heart will be also" (Matthew 6:21, NRSV).

While society frequently presents wealth as a measure of success and status, the Holy Scriptures invite us to see it as a means of stewardship, a resource to be managed wisely for God's purposes. Paul echoes this sentiment, encouraging believers to adopt a transformed perspective on wealth and possessions: "Do not be conformed to this world, but be transformed by the renewing of your minds, so that you may discern what is the will of God—what is good and acceptable and perfect" (Romans 12:2, NRSV). The way we manage our money is one way to reflect this transformed life and to demonstrate our trust in God's provision.

Misconceptions About Money and Faith

Several misconceptions persist within Christian communities regarding money, each impacting our spiritual lives and practices. Some common myths include:

1. **Money Itself is Evil:** A misinterpretation of Paul's words in 1 Timothy 6:10 has led some to believe that "money is the root of all evil." In reality, Paul states that "the love of money is a root of all kinds of evil" (NRSV). It's not money itself that is problematic, but an unhealthy attachment to it—when it becomes an idol or source of identity.

2. **Poverty is More Spiritual:** Some believe that wealth is inherently sinful and that poverty is a sign of greater spirituality. While Jesus did call the rich young ruler to sell his possessions (Matthew 19:21), this was not a blanket condemnation of wealth but an invitation to prioritize God above all else. Wealth or poverty in themselves are not spiritual virtues; it's our heart posture and how we use our resources that matter.

3. **Wealth is Proof of God's Favor:** Another common belief is that material wealth is a direct indication of God's blessing. Yet, throughout scripture, we see that both the wealthy and the poor can be faithful or unfaithful. God's blessing is not measured by material wealth but by a life aligned with God's will. Faithful stewardship is marked by generosity and a willingness to use our resources for the benefit of others.

4. **Money and Faith Should Be Separate:** Many Christians view financial matters as secular concerns that shouldn't intersect with faith. However, Jesus teaches that our resources are very much a part of our discipleship. Money can be a means of ministry, a tool for helping those in need, and a way to honor God when used responsibly and generously.

Wesleyan Teaching on Money

John Wesley's teachings on money are among the most practical and enduring in Christian history. In his sermon, "The Use of Money," Wesley provides a framework that invites us to view financial stewardship as a vital part of discipleship. Wesley's three guiding principles—earn all you can, save all you can, and give all you can—encourage a balanced, faithful approach to wealth.

1. **Earn All You Can:** Wesley believed that earning money was not only permissible but also important. However, he emphasized that we must earn in ways that honor God and do not harm ourselves or others. Wesley warned against work that damages physical or spiritual health or exploits others, urging believers to seek ethical ways to earn a living that reflect love for God and neighbor.

2. **Save All You Can:** Wesley's instruction to "save" did not mean accumulating wealth for personal security or status. Instead, he encouraged Methodists to avoid unnecessary spending and live simply. Saving allows us to avoid waste and to steward our resources responsibly, ensuring that what we have can be used for God's work rather than personal indulgence.

3. **Give All You Can:** For Wesley, the ultimate purpose of earning and saving was to give. He viewed all possessions as belonging to God and believed that wealth was given so we could help others. Wesley practiced what he preached, living simply and donating most of his income to charitable causes. His legacy of generosity challenges us to view our financial resources as tools for ministry, ways to uplift the poor, support the church, and bring God's kingdom closer to reality.[38]

Wesley's framework remains relevant today, challenging us to consider whether our financial practices align with our values. When we earn ethically, save mindfully, and give generously, we embody a faith that extends beyond words to action.

Money as a Means of Grace

Money, when understood in the context of discipleship, becomes a "means of grace." Wesleyan theology identifies "means of grace" as practices through which God's grace flows to us and through us to the world. When we manage our finances in ways that honor God, money becomes a channel for God's love, justice, and compassion. Through our giving, we participate in God's redemptive work, helping to meet the needs of the church, our community, and the broader world.

In giving, we also express trust in God's provision. Jesus instructs his followers not to be anxious about their needs, assuring them that "your heavenly Father knows that you need all these things" (Matthew 6:32, NRSV). Generosity, then, is an act of faith, a way to place our reliance on God rather than our wealth. This trust liberates us from the anxiety of scarcity and enables us to experience the joy of sharing in God's abundant love. Living out a vow of gifts calls us to approach finances with intentionality and faithfulness. Some practical steps to consider in cultivating financial stewardship include:

1. **Budget with Purpose:** A faith-centered budget reflects your values and commitments, prioritizing generosity, debt reduction, and mindful spending. By setting aside a portion of income for giving, we make generosity a regular, intentional practice rather than an afterthought.

2. **Align Spending with Values:** Consider how each purchase reflects your values. Are there ways to support ethical businesses, avoid waste, or invest in products that honor God's creation? Mindful spending helps us live out our faith in practical, everyday choices.

3. **Practice Generosity Regularly:** Whether through tithes, offerings, or charitable giving, regular generosity reminds us that everything we have comes from God. The church's mission, community organizations, and global ministries all rely on faithful giving to meet spiritual and material needs.

4. **Teach Financial Stewardship:** Conversations about money can be challenging, but teaching younger generations the principles of financial stewardship equips them to view money as a tool for serving God and others. This might include lessons on budgeting, saving, ethical earning, and the joy of giving.

5. **Reflect on Giving as Worship:** When we give, we are not merely making a financial transaction; we are engaging in worship. Giving connects us to the larger story of God's work in the world, allowing us to participate in transforming lives and communities. When we see our financial gifts as worship, we elevate the act of giving to an expression of faith.

Our approach to money is a critical part of our discipleship journey, shaping not only our finances but also our hearts. In the Gospel of Luke, Jesus emphasizes this, warning that "no one can serve two masters... You cannot serve God and wealth" (Luke 16:13, NRSV).

Jesus isn't condemning money itself; rather, he is pointing to the danger of letting wealth control our lives. Money, when viewed rightly, is a means to serve God's purposes—a tool that enables us to live out our faith through compassion, justice, and love.

Money matters not because it defines us but because it reflects our values. Through our approach to finances, we can live out our trust in God, embody Christ's generosity, and extend God's kingdom on earth. The vow of gifts challenges us to see our resources as an integral part of our faith, calling us to steward our finances in ways that honor God and serve our neighbor.

Reflection Questions:

1. What does financial stewardship mean to you, and how might it reflect your relationship with God?
2. In what ways does your spending or giving align with your values and faith? Are there areas where you feel called to make adjustments?
3. How might regular giving deepen your sense of connection to God and the community?
4. What would it look like to approach money as a means of grace, a way to experience and share God's love?
5. Are there financial habits or myths that you feel called to reconsider in light of faith-based stewardship?

Our Spiritual Gifts

> *Now there are different gifts, but the same Spirit. And there are different ministries, but the same Lord. And there are different results, but the same God who produces all of them in everyone. To each person the manifestation of the Spirit is given for the benefit of all.*
>
> — 1 CORINTHIANS 12:4-7, NET.

The topic of spiritual gifts has been a source of significant debate among theologians throughout church history. Different Christian traditions interpret spiritual gifts in varying ways, which has led to some controversial discussions.

ROOTED IN DISCIPLESHIP

These disagreements often focus on the nature of the gifts, whether they are still relevant today, and how they should be practiced within the church.

Our understanding of spiritual gifts is deeply tied to our understanding of God's grace and the transformative power of the Holy Spirit. For us, as United Methodists, spiritual gifts are not merely given to us for personal gain or pride, but they have been given to us by God to strengthen the church and further the reality of God's kingdom on earth. Spiritual gifts are a sign of God's love, an outpouring of grace that empowers believers to serve others, live holy lives, and build up the body of Christ.

One of the core principles we must understand is that spiritual gifts are a manifestation of God's grace in the lives of believers. These gifts have been given to Christians not because of our merit but because of God's unmerited love. Spiritual gifts, therefore, are a way for believers to experience and share God's grace.

Gifts like teaching, healing, prophecy, and service are ways in which the Holy Spirit worked in the lives of believers to accomplish God's purposes on earth. This reminds us that spiritual gifts are meant for the community of believers, that is, the church.

As the Apostle Paul points out in 1 Corinthians 12, just as the body needs different parts to function, the church needs a variety of spiritual gifts to carry out its mission. It would be impossible for the church to thrive unless each member uses their gifts to serve others. Spiritual gifts, whether they seem big or small, public or private, are all essential for the life and health of the church. No gift is more valuable than another; all are necessary in the body of Christ.

Spiritual Gifts of the Holy Spirit

The gifts of the Spirit are diverse and serve various functions. The New Testament lists a variety of gifts given by the Holy Spirit to believers. In 1 Corinthians 12, Paul describes gifts such as wisdom, knowledge, faith, healing, miracles, prophecy, distinguishing between spirits, speaking in tongues, and interpretation of tongues. Each gift is meant to build up the church and extend God's kingdom on earth.

> ➤ **Wisdom and Knowledge:** These gifts enable believers to understand God's will more deeply and to make decisions aligned with that will.
>
> ➤ **Healing and Miracles:** These gifts allow believers to act as instruments of God's healing and miraculous power in the world, showing the love and compassion of God.

- ➤ **Prophecy:** Prophecy helps the church remain faithful to God's voice, offering guidance and encouragement, calling the church to see hope in times of challenge, and seek redirection towards God's will.
- ➤ **Discernment:** The gift of distinguishing between spirits helps believers recognize truth from error, guiding the church in times of confusion or falsehood.
- ➤ **Tongues and Interpretation of Tongues:** These gifts are seen in many charismatic and Pentecostal traditions as powerful signs of God's presence, used for worship and edification of the church.

These gifts are not for personal benefit but are always intended for the edification of others, as Paul clearly states in 1 Corinthians 12:7. The church needs all of these gifts to be functioning properly in order to fulfill its mission. While some may be more prominent or visible than others, every gift is vital to the health and growth of the body of Christ.

Spiritual Gifts and Love

However, the use of these gifts has to be rooted in love. Love should be the driving force behind everything believers do, including the exercise of spiritual gifts. In his sermon, The Almost Christian, John Wesley highlights that spiritual gifts, no matter how powerful or impressive, are of no value without love. In fact, even gifts like prophecy and speaking in tongues are meaningless if they are not motivated by love. For Wesley, love is the highest virtue, and the use of spiritual gifts should always point back to love for God and neighbor.

This love-driven use of spiritual gifts is closely connected to our United Methodist doctrine of holiness. The gifts of the Spirit are not just for the individual's benefit but are part of our ongoing journey toward holiness. For us, holiness is not a distant goal but something that we are called to pursue daily. The gifts of the Spirit are tools that help us grow in holiness and serve others in love. They are gifts meant to shape our lives, not just demonstrate power.

John Wesley encouraged believers to pray for spiritual gifts. He believed that as the Holy Spirit moved within people, enabling them to be filled with more gifts, this was something to be actively pursued. This wasn't about striving to "earn" gifts or to outdo others, but rather about humbling oneself and asking God for gifts that would serve His kingdom and build up the body of Christ. In fact, Wesley suggested that it was the Holy Spirit that led individuals into the fullness of their calling, guiding them toward the specific gifts they would use in their lives.

ROOTED IN DISCIPLESHIP

Spiritual Gifts Assessment: A Tool for Discovery

As we reflect on our own spiritual gifts, it can be helpful to take an assessment or inventory to better understand the unique ways the Holy Spirit has equipped us for ministry. A spiritual gifts assessment can serve as a tool to help individuals discern their God-given gifts. These assessments are often based on biblical teachings and are designed to help believers reflect on their strengths and inclinations for service within the church.

Taking a spiritual gifts assessment can provide clarity about the gifts God has entrusted to us, whether they are gifts of leadership, service, teaching, encouragement, or something else. It helps us identify areas where we can most effectively serve others and contribute to the overall mission of the church. While these assessments can provide helpful insights, they are not meant to be prescriptive. Ultimately, the Holy Spirit is the one who empowers and directs us in the use of our gifts, and our response should always be one of humility and openness.

As United Methodists, we believe that everyone has been given gifts by the Spirit to serve the church and the world. By understanding and using our gifts, we participate in the great work that God is doing in the world. As we pray for guidance, seek out opportunities to use our gifts, and humbly serve others, we contribute to the flourishing of the body of Christ, growing together in holiness and love.

Reflection Questions:

> - What spiritual gifts do you recognize in your life, and how have you seen them used to serve others and build up the body of Christ?
> - How does the use of spiritual gifts in love (as emphasized by John Wesley) challenge you in how you serve others, both in the church and beyond?
> - In what ways can your spiritual gifts help you grow in holiness and align more closely with God's will for your life?
> - How can you intentionally seek to develop and use your spiritual gifts to contribute to the mission of the church and the kingdom of God?
> - Have you ever experienced a time when using your spiritual gifts felt particularly fulfilling? What can you learn from that experience to continue growing in your gifts?

What's That in Your Hand?

Exodus 4:2 shows us a simple and yet profound encounter between God and Moses. As Moses comes to terms with the reality of God's presence at the burning bush, he is called to go back to the place he had fled, to lead God's people to freedom. In the midst of their exchange, God asks Moses a simple question: "What's that in your hand?" Moses, standing before the burning bush, feels very unqualified, overwhelmed, and hesitant. God's question is an invitation to recognize the power of what he already possessed. This question—"What's that in your hand?"—reveals an essential truth: each of us has been endowed with unique gifts that, when offered in service to God, advance the divine purpose on earth and contribute to the liberation and flourishing of all creation. The gifts in our hands—our talents, passions, and abilities—are spiritual resources meant to be channeled into God's work in the world.

Theologian Howard Thurman, reminds us, "There is in every person, something that waits and listens for the sound of the genuine in herself…There is in you, something that waits and listens for the sound of the genuine in your self. Nobody like you has ever been born... And no one like you would ever be born again. You are the only one."[39]

When we consider our own calling, purpose, and vocation, we see that God's question to Moses is a question to each of us: "What's that in your hand?" This question invites us to look at our gifts as instruments through which God can work, no matter how humble or ordinary they may seem.

As we see in the lives of Moses, Gideon, Isaiah, Jeremiah, and others, God's call does not depend on our self-assessment or sense of readiness; it depends on our willingness to recognize our gifts and allow God to amplify them for a greater purpose.

Gifts and Calling in the Biblical Narrative

Throughout the Old Testament, God calls individuals in ways that reveal both the complexity and the power of spiritual gifts. These stories illustrate a classic pattern: a divine encounter, initial hesitation, divine reassurance, and ultimately, an obedient response. Each figure's call story reveals that God often uses what we already hold in our hands—our gifts, however hidden they may be—to fulfill a specific purpose.

1. **Moses (Exodus 3-4):** Moses, a shepherd in Midian, encounters God through the burning bush. Although he feels inadequate and slow of

speech, God reassures him and uses the staff in his hand as a symbol of divine power. The staff becomes a means through which God's liberation unfolds, reminding Moses that his ordinary tools and talents are potent in God's hands.

2. **Gideon (Judges 6):** Gideon, an unlikely hero, is called while hiding from the Midianites. When he questions his own strength and doubts God's presence with Israel, God reassures him: "I will be with you." Although Gideon is unsure, God uses him to deliver Israel, illustrating how God can work through our insecurities and transform our gifts into tools for justice.

3. **Isaiah (Isaiah 6):** Isaiah's vision in the temple brings him face to face with God's holiness. Although he feels unworthy, God purifies him and calls him to speak to the people. Isaiah's gift of prophetic vision becomes a means for God to guide, convict, and ultimately comfort the people, pointing to a time of restoration.

4. **Jeremiah (Jeremiah 1):** Jeremiah, called at a young age, doubts his ability to speak on behalf of God. Yet God assures him, touching his mouth and giving him the words to proclaim. Jeremiah's prophetic voice emerges from his initial hesitation, becoming a profound instrument of God's justice and compassion.

5. **Amos (Amos 7):** Amos is a shepherd and a farmer, not from a lineage of prophets, yet God calls him to speak against injustice in Israel. Amos's gifts and background bring a unique perspective to his prophetic message, reminding us that God often calls us to serve within the contexts and communities we know best.

6. **Samuel (1 Samuel 3):** Samuel, as a young boy, hears God calling him in the night. Initially confused, he learns to listen and respond, developing a gift for discerning God's voice. His life of faithful service as a prophet and judge shows how attentiveness to God's call can shape a life of transformative leadership.

Each of these individuals brings a unique set of gifts to their call. Moses' staff, Gideon's courage, Isaiah's vision, Jeremiah's words, Amos's knowledge of justice, and Samuel's listening heart are all "in their hands," available for God to use. In every case, these gifts contribute not only to personal transformation but also to the liberation, healing, and renewal of the broader community.

Gifts as Instruments of Liberation and Transformation

The question "What's that in your hand?" challenges us to see our gifts as integral to God's work of liberation. Moses's staff becomes a tool for liberation, a sign of God's power that confronts Pharaoh's empire and frees the people. Gideon's courage, though initially faint, becomes a gift through which God delivers Israel. Isaiah's prophetic words call for justice and hope, and Amos's message to the powerful challenges systemic injustice.

Each call story reminds us that the gifts we hold are not simply for our benefit but for the common good and for the liberation of all who are bound by oppression, fear, and despair.

In the Wesleyan tradition, spiritual gifts are considered means through which God's grace flows outward, transforming lives and communities. John Wesley, the founder of Methodism, taught that God's grace calls us to a life of "holiness of heart and life," where faith and works are inseparable.

Wesley believed that our gifts—whether practical skills, spiritual insights, or acts of compassion—are given to us to embody God's kingdom on earth, promoting justice, mercy, and love. Each gift contributes to the well-being of the community, becoming a force for collective liberation and healing.

Recognizing Purpose and Vocation

Our gifts, when recognized and embraced, reveal a sense of purpose and vocation. Vocation is not limited to a particular profession or job; it is the act of aligning our lives with God's purpose, responding to the call to love God and neighbor. This call to vocation is a call to partnership with God, to use our gifts for purposes that transcend personal gain or ambition. Instead, our gifts serve to build up the body of Christ and to contribute to the welfare of the world around us.

The Apostle Paul's words in Romans 12:6-8 emphasize the diversity of gifts within the body of Christ:

> "We have different gifts that are consistent with God's grace…If your gift is prophecy, you should prophesy…If your gift is service, devote yourself to serving."

These words remind us that each gift is a vital part of the community, meant to complement others and to serve the broader purposes of God's kingdom.

ROOTED IN DISCIPLESHIP

Embracing the Gifts We Hold

The call to embrace our gifts, as Moses did with his staff, is a call to trust that what we have is enough. We may feel inadequate, as Gideon did, or inexperienced, like Jeremiah. Yet God continually assures us: "I will be with you." Our gifts—whether they seem ordinary or extraordinary—are filled with potential when surrendered to God's purposes.

To ask ourselves, "What's that in your hand?" is to seek God's vision for our lives, to discern how our unique gifts can be channels for God's love, justice, and mercy.

These gifts, whether they are gifts of service, teaching, leadership, or compassion, are to be cherished and used in alignment with God's call. They may challenge systems of oppression, inspire hope, offer healing, or bring comfort. In every case, they serve as instruments through which God's kingdom takes root in the world.

The Call to Engage Fully

We are each called to offer our gifts fully, in ways that honor the divine image within us and work toward the liberation and flourishing of all creation. Just as Moses took up his staff, and just as the prophets embraced their callings, we are invited to respond with courage and generosity.

We are called to hold our gifts with open hands, willing to use them for God's purposes, knowing that in doing so, we join a long line of those who have worked for the welfare of the world around them.

In answering this call, we participate in a sacred purpose, allowing the gifts we hold to become blessings to others and signs of God's grace in a world in need.

Like Moses, Gideon, Isaiah, Jeremiah, Amos, and Samuel, we are given a unique opportunity to bring forth God's love and justice, contributing to the redemption and transformation of creation. And so, we ask ourselves again, "What's that in your hand?" and pray that we may offer it in faithful response to God's call.

Reflection Questions:

> ➢ What unique gifts, abilities, or passions has God placed in your hands, and how might you use them to serve others and honor God?

- Have you ever felt inadequate or hesitant to respond to God's call? How can you trust God to work through your gifts despite feelings of fear or doubt?
- How do your gifts align with God's mission of justice, mercy, and love in the world, and what steps can you take to live more fully into that purpose?
- How do your gifts complement those of others in your church or community, and how can you encourage others to recognize and use their own gifts?
- How do you create space to hear God's call in your life, and how can prayer and reflection help you discern the best ways to use your gifts?

Identifying our Gifts and Talents

The gifts we offer to God and the world are as unique and diverse as we are. Each of us has been endowed with talents, passions, and abilities that are meant to be discovered, nurtured, and shared. In the United Methodist tradition, our gifts are not only for personal fulfillment but are central to our calling as disciples that seek to grow the in love of God and in service to neighbors.

While there is a variety of gifts, we can organize them into three broad categories: the gifts of the head, the gifts of the hands, and the gifts of the heart. Together these form a holistic understanding of how God equips us for lives of service, justice, and compassion.

This exercise is deeply rooted in the principles of Asset-Based Community Development (ABCD), which emphasizes identifying and mobilizing the existing strengths, talents, and resources within a community rather than focusing on its deficiencies.

This model of community development invites us to see our gifts—no matter how ordinary they may seem—as vital assets for building stronger communities. As John P. Kretzmann and John L. McKnight, pioneers of ABCD, state in their foundational work, *Building Communities from the Inside Out,* "Every single person has capacities, abilities, and gifts. Living a good life depends on whether those capacities can be used, abilities expressed, and gifts given."[40] This approach aligns seamlessly with the biblical understanding that God has already equipped each of us with what we need to contribute to the flourishing of creation.

ROOTED IN DISCIPLESHIP

- ➢ **Gifts of the Head** represent our knowledge, intellect, and unique insights. These are the ways we think, plan, and create, contributing to the growth and flourishing of our communities.
- ➢ **Gifts of the Hands** involve our practical skills and abilities. These are the talents that allow us to build, care, and act in ways that bring tangible support to others.
- ➢ **Gifts of the Heart** encompass our deepest passions and desires. These are the areas where our emotions, values, and personal calling intersect, inspiring us to act on behalf of causes and people we care about most.

The Head, Hands, and Heart Exercise invites you to reflect on these gifts and consider how they align with God's purpose for your life. Just as God asked Moses, "What's that in your hand?" (Exodus 4:2), this exercise challenges us to identify what we already hold and how those gifts can be used for the greater good. It reminds us that the strengths we bring as individuals are not isolated but interconnected, forming a tapestry of gifts that can transform our faith communities and the world around us.

This process is not simply an inventory of skills or passions—it is a method of discernment. It asks us to look inward and upward, discovering how our unique combination of gifts can contribute to God's ongoing work of liberation, healing, and restoration in the world. By identifying these gifts, we recognize the ways in which God's grace flows through us and find opportunities to participate in building up the body of Christ.

Keep in mind that no gift is too small or insignificant. Whether it's a thoughtful idea, a skilled hand, or a passionate heart, every gift is an offering to God and a way to bless the world.

Gifts of the Head

These are intellectual and knowledge-based gifts that allow you to think critically, solve problems, and create solutions that benefit others. Gifts of the head often involve skills you've learned, areas of expertise, or insights that help you lead, educate, and support those around you.

They include:

1. **Analytical Thinking and Problem-Solving:** You have a gift for assessing situations and finding effective solutions. This could involve serving

GIFTS

on a church committee to address community needs, providing guidance on complex issues, or helping organizations streamline their processes.

2. **Knowledge of Scripture and Theology:** You enjoy studying the Bible and exploring theological concepts. This gift can be used by leading Bible studies, teaching Sunday school, or providing insight into faith questions for others seeking to grow spiritually.

3. **Research and Writing Skills:** You are skilled at gathering information and clearly communicating ideas. This might involve writing devotionals, preparing educational materials, contributing to church publications, or even assisting with grant writing for non-profits.

4. **Leadership and Vision:** You have the ability to see the big picture and inspire others toward shared goals. This gift could be used by serving in church leadership, guiding new ministries, or mentoring others in the community to develop their own gifts.

5. **Teaching and Educating:** You are skilled at explaining complex ideas in understandable ways. This gift could be used in adult education classes, tutoring children, or leading training sessions in various skills.

6. **Financial and Strategic Planning:** You have a talent for understanding finances, budgets, and planning for the future. This could lead you to serve on church finance teams, help families with budgeting skills, or provide financial counseling to those in need.

7. **Knowledge in Science, Health, or Medicine:** You have expertise in health, wellness, or medical fields. This gift can allow you to organize health screenings, provide health education, or offer wellness workshops within the community.

8. **Cross-Cultural Knowledge and Language Skills:** You are fluent in other languages or have experience with different cultures. This gift could be used to bridge cultural gaps, assist in translation for non-English speakers, or lead mission efforts in diverse communities.

9. **Public Speaking and Communication:** You have a talent for speaking clearly and connecting with audiences. This gift could be used to deliver sermons, lead workshops, advocate for social justice issues, or simply offer encouragement to groups.

10. **Technical and Analytical Knowledge:** You possess specialized knowledge in fields like technology, engineering, or data analysis.

This might involve volunteering to help with church technology needs, advising on infrastructure projects, or using data insights to help organizations make informed decisions.

11. **Organizational and Project Management Skills:** You are skilled in organizing projects and managing tasks effectively. This gift could be used to coordinate events, run church programs smoothly, or assist in organizing community outreach efforts.

Reflection:

Consider the areas of knowledge or intellectual abilities you have—what fields or topics do you feel passionate about? Where do you excel in understanding, teaching, or leading? Think about how you might use these gifts of the head to empower others, contribute to meaningful projects, and support the missions of your church and community. When shared, these gifts can bring clarity, wisdom, and direction to the body of Christ.

Gifts of the Hand

These are practical skills or abilities that you can use to serve others in tangible ways. Gifts of the hand are often talents you've developed over time or natural skills that allow you to make a direct impact in the lives of others in your community.

They include:

1. **Construction and Repair:** You have a knack for building, fixing, or repairing things. This could mean volunteering for Habitat for Humanity, helping with church maintenance, or assisting elderly neighbors with home repairs.

2. **Cooking and Hospitality:** You enjoy preparing meals and creating welcoming environments. This gift might lead you to cook for community events, deliver meals to those in need, or help with church hospitality during special gatherings.

3. **Artistic and Creative Skills:** You are talented in areas like painting, music, photography, or crafting. These skills can be used to create uplifting art for the community, volunteer to teach art classes, or provide creative contributions to church events and outreach.

4. **Organizing and Planning:** You are skilled at bringing order and structure to projects or events. This gift could allow you to coordinate church activities, organize community drives, or help families and individuals in need of logistical support.

5. **Gardening and Landscaping:** You have a green thumb and love working with plants. This might involve creating community gardens, maintaining church grounds, or helping neighbors beautify their spaces, contributing to a sense of peace and natural beauty.

6. **Teaching and Tutoring:** You have a gift for explaining concepts and guiding others in learning. You may volunteer to teach Sunday School, tutor children, or offer skills training for adults seeking employment.

7. **Craftsmanship and Design:** You are skilled in areas like carpentry, sewing, knitting, or other crafts. These hands-on gifts could lead you to create items for those in need, make blankets for the sick, or contribute to mission projects that require handmade goods.

8. **Technology and Media Skills:** You are comfortable with technology and enjoy helping others navigate it. This might involve running tech for worship services, setting up computer labs, or assisting seniors in learning how to use smartphones and computers.

9. **Transportation and Logistics:** You are able to assist with transportation needs or manage the logistics of moving people and resources. This might include driving people to appointments, organizing community outreach events, or delivering supplies to those in need.

10. **Financial and Administrative Skills:** You have skills in budgeting, accounting, or administrative tasks. These gifts might enable you to help families with financial planning, volunteer for church financial committees, or assist non-profits with bookkeeping.

Reflection:

Think about the practical abilities and skills you have—what comes easily to you, and where do you see your talents making a positive difference? How might you use these gifts of the hand to serve others, help your community, and honor God? Each practical skill is a valuable tool that, when shared, becomes a blessing to those around you.

Gifts of the Heart

These are things that stir a deep passion within you—causes or concerns that resonate so strongly that they compel you to take action. Gifts of the heart are the things that keep you awake at night or fill you with energy and purpose.

They may include:
1. **Advocacy for Justice:** You have a strong desire to see fairness and equity in the world. This could mean working for social justice, advocating for marginalized communities, or standing up against injustice in all its forms.
2. **Compassion for the Poor and Vulnerable:** You feel a deep empathy for those who struggle with poverty, homelessness, or illness. This passion might lead you to volunteer in shelters, mentor youth in underserved areas, or support healthcare initiatives for vulnerable populations.
3. **Environmental Stewardship:** A love for God's creation drives you to protect the earth. You may advocate for sustainable practices, lead recycling programs, support conservation efforts, or educate others about caring for the planet.
4. **Mentorship and Encouragement:** You are passionate about supporting others in their growth. This might mean mentoring young people, offering guidance to those in need, or simply being present for someone going through a difficult time.
5. **Care for the Sick and Grieving:** You feel called to walk alongside those experiencing illness or loss. Your heart's gift may lead you to serve in hospitals, become a hospice volunteer, or provide support to families dealing with grief.
6. **Hospitality and Welcoming:** You deeply value creating inclusive and welcoming spaces for others. This could involve opening your home to those in need, offering a warm welcome at church, or helping newcomers feel a sense of belonging in your community.
7. **Commitment to Education and Learning:** You believe in the power of knowledge to transform lives. This passion may lead you to support educational initiatives, teach, tutor, or mentor, helping others gain the skills they need to succeed.

8. **Empowering the Voiceless:** You have a heart for amplifying the voices of those who are often unheard. This might involve working with refugees, advocating for the disabled, or championing the rights of those often overlooked by society.

Reflection:

Think about the issues or causes that ignite a sense of purpose within you. How might you channel these gifts of the heart in ways that serve others and glorify God? Each passion is a unique calling, designed to make a lasting impact on the world around you.

> THEN THE KING WILL REPLY TO THEM, 'I ASSURE YOU THAT WHEN YOU HAVE DONE IT FOR ONE OF THE LEAST OF THESE BROTHERS AND SISTERS OF MINE, YOU HAVE DONE IT FOR ME.

— MATTHEW 25:40, CEB

PART 5
SERVICE
Embodying Christ's Love

Introduction

The vow of service calls us to embody Christ's love through acts of service, both within the church and in the wider community. Service is a central part of discipleship, reflecting Jesus' command to love our neighbors as ourselves. As members of the body of Christ, we are called to serve others with humility, compassion, and a heart for justice.

In Matthew 25, Jesus gives us a startling image of final judgment. The scene does not focus on creeds or confessions, but on concrete acts of compassion: feeding the hungry, clothing the naked, visiting the imprisoned, and welcoming the stranger. In this passage, Jesus identifies so fully with the poor and the vulnerable that to serve them is to serve Christ himself. This text does not negate the importance of belief or doctrine—far from it—but it does root the authenticity of our faith in acts of love. For followers of Jesus in the Wesleyan tradition, this is no peripheral idea; it is the very heart of discipleship.

Service is not an extracurricular activity for the committed few. Service are tangible acts of love and mercy that enables the gospel become visible in the world. Service is the embodied response of a people who have experienced grace.

ROOTED IN DISCIPLESHIP

Rooted in our baptismal identity and sustained by the example of Christ, who came not to be served but to serve, the vow of service is an expression of what Wesleyans call "social holiness"—a key conviction that true faith is always lived out in relationship with others. As John Wesley once wrote, "The gospel of Christ knows of no religion but social; no holiness but social holiness."[41] For Wesley, service was not just the fruit of a sanctified life—it was the means by which holiness was formed and made visible in the world.

To live out our vow of service is to take seriously God's mission of justice, peace, and healing. Wesley taught that discipleship requires both personal piety and public compassion.[42] When rightly understood, service is also an act of resistance against systems of exploitation we encounter in the world.[43] It is a way of participating in what some theologians call the divine economy of grace[44]—a radical reordering of community grounded in abundance, mutuality, and care. In this way, every act of service becomes a testimony to the transforming power of our Triune God.

So when we speak of "service," we do not merely mean volunteering at an event or completing a task. We mean offering our lives in response to the needs of others. We mean showing up with empathy, advocacy, and compassion. Not only that, but we mean listening, accompanying, giving, and standing in solidarity. The vow of service calls us to embrace a lifestyle that reflects the pattern of Jesus: self-giving love that crosses boundaries and lifts burdens.

The church provides many ways for each person to live out this vow—through ministries of care, local outreach, and global mission partnerships. A healthy discipleship system equips every member with regular opportunities to serve others, recognizing that when we serve, we are not only helping our neighbors—we are meeting Christ in them.

Through service, we become Christ's hands and feet in the world. Our actions become a form of worship, a visible sign of the invisible grace at work within us. As we walk the path of discipleship, this vow challenges us to grow in humility, courage, **and compassion—living lives that reflect the love of Jesus Christ.**

REFLECTION QUESTIONS:

> ➤ What emotions or thoughts rise within you when you consider your role in serving others?
>
> ➤ Where do you feel drawn—or perhaps stretched—when you think about being Christ's hands and feet?

SERVICE

- What opportunities for service within your church or community excite or challenge you?
- How might God be inviting you to grow or step outside your comfort zone through acts of service?
- What does the idea of service mean to you in this season of life?
- How is God shaping your understanding of what it means to serve others with humility and joy?

Service As Wesleyan Discipleship

Blessed Are the Poor

From its earliest days, the Methodist movement was defined by its deep and abiding concern for the poor. As Richard Heitzenrater notes in *The Poor and the People Called Methodists*, John Wesley's evangelistic ministry among coal miners, laborers, widows, and the working poor was not incidental—it was central to the movement's identity.

The Methodists were not a church of the powerful but a people in solidarity with the marginalized. They visited prisoners, organized health clinics, established lending funds, and developed schools for poor children. The movement did not simply preach to the poor—it lived with them, among them, and often as them.

Wesley viewed poverty through the lens of prevenient grace. All persons, regardless of status, bear the image of God and are recipients of divine love.[45] This theological affirmation compelled Wesley and his followers to enter into active relationships with the poor—not to dispense charity from a distance, but to be mutually transformed through love and care. In fact, Wesley insisted that the poor were often more spiritually receptive and more capable of teaching others about the gospel than the wealthy.[46]

This theology was not abstract. Wesley built it into the very fabric of Methodist life. Acts of mercy—feeding the hungry, clothing the naked, visiting the sick and imprisoned—were considered means of grace. In the same way that prayer, communion, and Scripture reading opened believers to the presence of God, so too did serving the poor.

ROOTED IN DISCIPLESHIP

In his sermon "The Scripture Way of Salvation," Wesley made clear that good works do not earn salvation, but they are the fruit of grace and channels through which God's sanctifying power flows.

Thus, the vow of service is not an add-on to spiritual growth. It is a vehicle of sanctification. Wesley would argue that we cannot become holy without acts of mercy, and the poor are not merely recipients of our kindness but partners in our formation. Service, in this light, becomes not only ethical but sacramental.

Practical Divinity: Faith Working Through Love

John Wesley often described his theological vision as "practical divinity,"[47] meaning a theology that is lived out in everyday faithfulness, where belief and behavior are inseparably linked, and the goal of doctrine is the transformation of both heart and life. Wesley's interest was not in constructing speculative doctrine but in fostering transformed lives. In sermon after sermon, he emphasized that Christian belief must be lived.[48] Faith without works, he said, is not only dead—it is false.[49] Wesley's methodical spirituality was built on the conviction that love of God must lead to tangible and practical love of neighbor, especially the poor, the sick, and the forgotten.

This integration of belief and action was rooted in his doctrine of grace. Salvation is not merely a private assurance of heaven; it is the beginning of a new life infused with divine love.[50] For Wesley, grace is not static or abstract—it is dynamic and relational, initiating a lifelong journey of transformation. Prevenient grace goes before us, awakening our conscience, drawing us toward God, and enabling even our first inclinations to respond in faith. Justifying grace brings forgiveness and peace with God, but it is sanctifying grace that propels the believer toward holy living in the world. Holiness of heart must become holiness of life, expressed in concrete practices that embody God's justice and mercy.

Jesus in the Gospel of Matthew calls his followers to a righteousness that exceeds mere legalism, urging them to care for the poor, love their enemies, and seek first the kingdom of God (Matthew 5–7). Like the upside down kingdom of God, where the first are last and the humble are exalted, taught by Jesus, Wesley's theology offers a radical view of discipleship as it calls us to see personal piety (the work of grace in the soul) and social responsibility (participation in God's mission) as indivisible realities for mature faith.

In this framework, service is no longer just an act of kindness. It is a theologically charged participation in the life of God. It resists the individualism and

SERVICE

commodification that dominate modern society and reorients us toward community, dignity, and mutual flourishing. Service reflects the rhythm of the divine life itself: a life marked by self-giving, communion, and the building up of the household of God. Wesley's insistence on the social dimensions of salvation reminds us that to be holy is to be relational—to live and serve within God's grace-filled economy of love and justice.

A People Called to Serve

John Wesley's understanding of the Church was inseparable from its mission in the world. He did not view the Church as a retreat for the spiritually elite, but as a people set apart for service.[51] The Church exists not for its own preservation but for the transformation of the world. In his sermon "On Zeal," Wesley calls the Church to be marked by "zeal for works of mercy," reminding us that Christian witness is incomplete without a lived demonstration of God's compassion and justice.[52]

This view defines the Church by its commitment to helping others. As the Body of Christ, the Church is called to embody Christ's presence in the world, offering healing, hope, and reconciliation. The Church is not simply a gathering of individuals seeking spiritual growth; it is a community formed for the sake of others. United Methodists affirm that the Church is both sign and instrument of God's kingdom—a foretaste of the new creation God is bringing into being.[53]

As a community of faith, we take this identity seriously. Our worship, teaching, and fellowship are not ends in themselves—they are practices that form us for service. Every ministry, from children's programs to pastoral care to administrative leadership, exists to equip the body of Christ to serve others in love. When the Church serves, it reveals its truest nature: a community drawn into the life of Christ and sent out for the sake of the world.

A People Sent in Love

The early Methodist movement did not stop at preaching or personal devotion. The strength and genius of this movement was centered in structures that cultivated deep relationships and mutual responsibility—most notably, the class meeting. These small gatherings, usually composed of ten to twelve people who met weekly for prayer, spiritual reflection, testimony, and accountability. Yet beyond their spiritual intent, they functioned as engines of care, solidarity, and communal service.

ROOTED IN DISCIPLESHIP

Members of a class were expected to care for one another in both spiritual and tangible ways. They pooled resources to support widows, orphans, and the sick. They offered loans, delivered meals, visited the homebound, and ensured no member suffered in isolation. These acts of love were not seen as extraordinary; they were expected. Service was not the responsibility of a few—it was the shared rhythm of discipleship.

In this model, ministry was decentralized. Laypeople became active agents of grace in their neighborhoods. These structures allowed Methodists to live out Wesley's imperative: "Do all the good you can, by all the means you can... to all the people you can."[54] It was a radical democratization of ministry, grounded in the conviction that every follower of Christ is called to serve.

This model remains instructive today. Faith communities are called to embody this vision through small groups, care ministries, and outreach efforts. Service is not relegated to programs or committees—it is the shared vocation of the whole body of Christ. When we serve one another in love, we reclaim our heritage and practice a form of discipleship that is relational, mutual, and transformative.

Wesleyan discipleship is inherently missional. It sees the church not as a refuge from the world, but as a participant in God's mission of justice, healing, and grace. To serve one another is to participate in the divine life, to recognize Christ in our neighbor, and to become instruments of God's peace in the world. In this tradition, service is not merely something we do—it is the shape love takes as it moves through us into the world.

Sacramental Service

Wesleyan theology has long emphasized the presence of God in the ordinary means of grace: prayer, Scripture, the Lord's Supper, and acts of mercy. In this tradition, service is holy encounter. When we feed the hungry, visit the sick, clothe the naked, or comfort the grieving, we are participating in something sacred. These moments are not peripheral to our faith; they are liturgical. They are embodied expressions of God's grace and signs of the coming kingdom.

This sacramental vision reframes our understanding of everyday acts of compassion. In serving others, we meet Christ himself (Matthew 25:40). A bowl of soup becomes a vessel of divine mercy. A visit to a nursing home becomes an encounter with God's presence. A shared meal becomes communion. These moments blur the line between sacred and secular, reminding us that God's grace saturates the world and meets us in human need.

SERVICE

Service, in this light, becomes a form of liturgy—a rhythm of giving and receiving through which God forms us and blesses the world. As we serve, we are not only agents of grace but recipients of it. We are changed by those we serve. We are drawn deeper into the mystery of God's love.

In the life of the Church, acts of service are not merely tasks to complete—they are holy opportunities to encounter Christ. Whether preparing communion, tutoring a child, delivering meals, or writing cards of encouragement, each act becomes an offering. Service becomes sacramental when it is offered in love, grounded in prayer, and oriented toward Christ.

Reflection Questions:

- Have you ever experienced an act of service as a moment of holy encounter?
- How does thinking of service as sacramental change your posture or motivation?
- What ordinary acts in your life might become holy when done in love?
- In what ways are you experiencing or offering care within your community of faith?
- How does your understanding of the Church shape your call to serve?
- How might your small group or ministry team serve one another more intentionally?
- What aspects of church life most clearly reflect the Church's mission to serve the world?
- What does it mean for you to embrace service as a shared vocation, rather than a personal choice?
- Where do you see God calling our church to deepen its culture of mutual care?
- How might reclaiming the spirit of the class meeting transform the way you serve, lead, and live?
- How might our congregation grow in its identity as a community formed for others?

ROOTED IN DISCIPLESHIP

A Trinitarian Framework for Service

As we have established, Christian service is not merely an ethical obligation or an expression of kindness. Christian service, at its heart, is participation in the life of God—a divine life marked by communion, mission, and self-giving love. To understand service in this way is to root it not in human effort, but in the very being of God. The act of serving becomes a reflection of the God we worship, whose own life is eternally relational and generative.

This vision finds its deepest grounding in the doctrine of the Trinity—one God in three persons: Father, Son, and Holy Spirit. The Trinity is not an abstract puzzle to be solved but a living reality to be experienced. A reality that reveals the essence of divine love. God the Father, in love, sends the Son. The Son, in humility, gives his life for the world. The Spirit, in power, animates the church to continue Christ's mission. This is a God who gives, sends, and shares—a God whose life is poured out in love for others.

When we serve, we step into this divine rhythm. We do not merely imitate God's love; we participate in it. The Father sends us in love, just as he sent the Son (John 20:21). The Son's pattern of service—healing the sick, feeding the hungry, and washing feet—becomes our own. The Holy Spirit empowers us to carry this mission into the world with boldness and grace. Service becomes, then, a participation in the divine life and a visible witness to God's ongoing work of redemption.

This framework challenges us to view service not only as action, but as formation. When we serve, we are shaped by the relational, giving nature of God. We begin to love as God loves: generously, vulnerably, and with attention to those the world overlooks. Service is a crucible of spiritual formation, where we learn humility, patience, and dependence on the Spirit. In serving, we draw near to the heart of God.

The church, as the Body of Christ, is called to reflect the communal and self-giving nature of the Trinity. As United Methodists, we affirm that the church exists for the sake of the world—to be a sign, foretaste, and instrument of God's kingdom.

Our acts of mercy, justice, and compassion are not peripheral to the gospel; they are the embodied witness of a people living in communion with the Triune God. In this divine economy of grace, service is not about scarcity, control, or merit. It is about abundance, mutual care, and the free flow of love.

SERVICE

As followers of Christ, we seek to root our ministries of service in a Trinitarian vision. Whether feeding the hungry, comforting the grieving, or advocating for justice, we do not serve alone. We participate in the life of God—empowered by the Spirit, following the example of Christ, and glorifying the Father. This is the holy mystery of service: that in giving ourselves away, we discover the joy and fullness of life in God.

Reflection Questions:
- How does viewing service as participation in God's life shape your understanding of discipleship?
- Where in your life or ministry have you experienced the Spirit's empowerment for service?
- In what ways does your community reflect the self-giving love of the Triune God?
- How might your acts of service become more worshipful, intentional, and relational?
- What practices help you stay rooted in God's love as you serve others?

Three Arenas of Service: In-Church, Local Outreach, and Global Mission

The vow of service is both deeply personal and profoundly communal. It arises from the transformative work of God's grace in our lives and leads us outward to respond in love. This outward movement of grace takes shape in multiple contexts, each one an opportunity to express the love of Christ in tangible ways. Service begins in the heart, but it cannot remain there. It grows in the shared life of the church and stretches beyond the sanctuary into the world, becoming a visible expression of the kingdom of God. When we serve, we reflect the character of the God who sends, gives, and redeems. We live out our discipleship not in isolation, but in connection—with fellow believers, with our neighbors, and with the global body of Christ.

United Methodists understand discipleship as a life shaped by grace and lived in response to the needs of others.[55] Our service, therefore, touches every aspect of our lives, calling us to act as Christ's hands and feet in three essential arenas: in-church service, local outreach, and global mission. These dimensions are not separate callings but interwoven expressions of one life of love.

ROOTED IN DISCIPLESHIP

In-Church Service: Discipleship in Community

Service within the church is the foundation of Christian community. It reflects Paul's vision in *1 Corinthians 12*, where each member is a part of the Body of Christ, with unique gifts given for the common good. John Wesley emphasized the communal and embodied nature of holiness, describing the church not merely as a gathering of individuals, but as a living organism of grace. Each believer is a vital part of the whole—"If one member suffers, all suffer together; if one member is honored, all rejoice together" (1 Cor. 12:26, ESV).

In-church service takes many forms: leading worship as liturgists or musicians; teaching children, youth, and adults in Sunday School or small groups; offering hospitality as greeters, ushers, or fellowship hosts; providing care ministries to the sick, grieving, or homebound; supporting worship through media and sound technology; serving communion or assisting with altar preparation; or participating in administrative and spiritual leadership through committees and teams.

These ministries are not peripheral; they are the very heartbeat of the church. They create a sacred rhythm of giving and receiving that shapes a culture of discipleship.

Every task, whether seen or unseen, contributes to the health and vitality of the congregation. Wesley's holistic ecclesiology reminds us that grace is not merely something we receive privately, but something we embody communally.

Serving together deepens trust, fosters belonging, and cultivates spiritual growth. In-church service is not just preparation for mission; it *is* mission. It is where we practice the habits of prayer, presence, gifts, service, and witness in a supportive environment before carrying them into the world.

Reflection Questions:
- ➢ What role do you feel called to play in building up the Body of Christ?
- ➢ How does serving within your church community deepen your faith and discipleship?
- ➢ In what ways can you offer your gifts to support others in their spiritual journey?

Local Outreach: Neighborliness and Justice

Jesus' command to love our neighbor is most readily practiced in the communities where we live. Local outreach invites us to step beyond the church

SERVICE

walls and into the lives of our neighbors—to listen, to walk alongside, and to advocate for their flourishing. This model of relational ministry reflects Jesus' own pattern of drawing near to those on the margins, restoring their dignity through presence and compassion.

Many congregations embody this call through partnerships with local schools, shelters, food pantries, and community organizations.

Through mentoring programs, home repair initiatives, meal preparation, and advocacy efforts, the church seeks to meet real needs while also addressing the systemic causes of injustice.

However, not all forms of helping are truly helpful. Drawing from *When Helping Hurts* by Steve Corbett and Brian Fikkert and *Helping Without Hurting in Church Benevolence*, we learn that healthy service avoids creating dependency or reinforcing power imbalances. Instead, it empowers, restores, and honors the agency of those served. Effective outreach begins with *listening*—not assuming what others need but asking, learning, and forming mutual relationships.

As Chris Batey highlights in *Jesus and the Poor*, authentic ministry with the poor requires us to see Christ in the faces of our neighbors and recognize our shared need for grace.

Local outreach becomes transformative not only for those served but for those serving. It reshapes our assumptions, deepens our empathy, and enlarges our sense of community.

Reflection Questions:
- Who is your neighbor, and how are you being called to love them?
- Where in your local community do you see Christ inviting you to respond?
- How can you move from transactional help to transformational relationships?

Global Mission: From Church to the World

The gospel is good news for the whole world. Jesus' parting words to his disciples were to be witnesses "in Jerusalem, in all Judea and Samaria, and to the ends of the earth" (*Acts 1:8*).

ROOTED IN DISCIPLESHIP

As members of a connectional church, United Methodists have both the structure and the calling to engage in global mission—participating in ministries of mercy, justice, and evangelism across continents and cultures.

This takes shape through short-term mission trips that build long-term relationships, financial support of global relief and development efforts, and partnerships with organizations that provide sustainable aid during times of crisis. Through such efforts, congregations participate in God's mission of healing, hope, and transformation around the world.

Global mission challenges us to think beyond charity. As M. Douglas Meeks notes, true Christian service resists the forces of global economic injustice by promoting solidarity, justice, and peace. Our giving and going should not reinforce cycles of poverty or colonial attitudes, but instead foster mutuality, empowerment, and long-term change. Global mission is less about what we do for others and more about what we do *with* others in God's global community.

We learn from the church in other cultures: their resilience, joy, worship, and hope. These relationships expand our theology and stretch our vision of the kingdom of God. Even if we never travel internationally, we participate in global mission through our prayers, offerings, advocacy, and awareness of how our everyday choices affect people around the world.

Reflection Questions:
- How does your understanding of God expand when you engage with the global church?
- What global issues stir your heart, and how might God be calling you to respond?
- In what ways can you participate in global mission even from your own community?

Formation through Service

Service is not merely something we do for others; it is a means through which God reshapes us. In God's work of grace within us, action is never one-directional. When we step into roles of caregiving, advocacy, or mission, we often find that the greatest transformation occurs within our hearts.

Over a decade ago, I traveled to Mozambique for a missional immersion experience. Mozambique is a stunningly beautiful country that, like many

SERVICE

post-colonial nations, continues to bear the scars of systemic injustice—centuries of colonization and decades of civil war. During my time there, I encountered the painful realities of a people whose hope for a better future rested not on governmental infrastructure or social programs, but on the transforming power of Jesus Christ.

As I walked alongside our Mozambican brothers and sisters, I saw more clearly the depth of poverty, the deplorable state of the local hospital, the absence of safe running water, and the weight of suffering borne by so many. And yet, in the midst of it all, I recalled John Wesley's words upon returning to England from America: *"I went to America to convert the Indians, but, O! who shall convert me?"*[56] The comfort and encouragement I thought I was bringing to others was quickly turned around and directed toward my own soul. I began to realize that addressing the brokenness of the world requires more than writing a check or launching another program. It requires a heart that is tender to the pain of others, a willingness to learn from those with no material goods to offer, and a humility to admit that we do not have all the answers. Above all, it requires the deep and difficult acknowledgment that transformation is not ours to engineer—it belongs to God alone.

While there, I witnessed the extraordinary work of Iris Ministries across Mozambique, but what struck me most was the faithful response of hundreds of individuals who had left behind homes, families, jobs, and comforts to answer God's call to ministry. One story that will always remain with me is that of Victorino Januário, a fourth-year student pastor. Victorino left his pregnant wife behind to complete his studies in Pemba. While there, he missed the birth of his first child, contracted malaria, and faced an uncertain future with no clear plan for income upon returning home. Yet when I asked how he was coping, he replied with calm assurance: "I don't know what the future holds, but I know God has a plan for my life. The same God who made a way for me to be in school will make a way for everything else."

That moment—and many others like it—deepened my understanding that what the world needs is not merely another initiative. It needs disciples: people willing to place their faith in Christ and follow his command to *"go and make disciples of all nations."* People willing to cross social, cultural, and economic boundaries to embody the love of Christ in a hurting world.

And this is precisely what *formation through service* looks like. Whether we find ourselves in Mozambique, Brazil, Clarksville, or anywhere else, the call remains the same: to move with compassion into action and to join God in healing what is broken.

When we serve, we are being discipled. We are learning to see with the eyes of Christ and to love with the heart of Christ. In every act of mercy and justice, the Holy Spirit stretches us, softens us, and sanctifies us—shaping us not only into those who serve, but into those who are being continually formed by the grace of God.

Reflection Questions: Formation through Service

- ➢ When have you stepped into a service opportunity expecting to give—and ended up receiving something unexpected in return?
- ➢ How has serving others changed the way you see God? Yourself? The world?
- ➢ What are some "holy moments" you've experienced while serving others—times when you sensed Christ's presence in surprising ways?
- ➢ Victorino expressed trust in God despite an uncertain future. When have you experienced (or struggled with) that kind of faith? What did you learn?
- ➢ This chapter emphasizes that true service is not just about writing a check or completing a task. What's the difference between transactional help and transformational discipleship?
- ➢ In what ways have you seen service lead to greater humility, compassion, or spiritual growth in your own life?
- ➢ Where in your community do you see deep need or brokenness? How might God be calling you to step in—not as a savior, but as a servant?
- ➢ How do you discern where God is already at work—and how do you decide whether or how to join in?
- ➢ How does this story from Mozambique challenge or expand your understanding of Jesus' call to "go and make disciples of all nations"?
- ➢ In your context (e.g., neighborhood, workplace, congregation), what barriers—cultural, social, economic—might God be calling you to cross for the sake of love?
- ➢ Reflect on this statement: *"When we serve, we are being discipled."* In what ways has service been a means of your spiritual formation?
- ➢ Which fruit of the Spirit (Galatians 5:22-23) do you see growing in your life as a result of serving others? Which one might God be inviting you to cultivate more deeply?

SERVICE

Reflection as a Spiritual Discipline

Transformation through service does not happen by accident. It must be nurtured through intentional reflection—a spiritual discipline that is too often overlooked in our action-oriented world. Without reflection, we risk confusing movement with meaning and busyness with holiness.

After each major service initiative—whether a Habitat for Humanity build or a community food drive—we gather in small groups to reflect. We ask:

- ➢ Where did you sense God's presence?
- ➢ What did you learn about yourself?
- ➢ What did you see in the community that broke your heart—or gave you hope?

These simple questions help integrate our thoughts, emotions, and actions. They create space for the Spirit to reveal what is being formed in us—not just what we did for others, but what God is doing within us.

We also encourage journaling as part of our discipleship rhythm. Some write by hand; others use digital tools like the Notes app on their phones. One youth reflected, "I didn't realize how much the refugee kids we helped reminded me of Jesus until I wrote it down."

Another formative tool we've adopted is the Examen, an ancient Ignatian practice of prayerful reflection. After a service experience, we often ask:

- ➢ Where today did I feel most alive?
- ➢ Where did I feel resistant, distant, or closed off?
- ➢ How might God be inviting me to grow?

These practices require no theological degree—only the willingness to pause, notice, and listen. In this way, reflection becomes a form of worship. It is an act of discipleship in itself, an acknowledgment that God is not only working *through* us, but also *within* us, shaping our hearts for love.

Service as a School of the Spirit

John Wesley famously declared, *"There is no holiness but social holiness."* This was not a slogan—it was a theological conviction rooted in his understanding of sanctification. Holiness, for Wesley, was never meant to be an individual pursuit. It is cultivated in relationship—with God and with others, especially those on the margins of society.

ROOTED IN DISCIPLESHIP

The early Methodist movement thrived not just in sanctuaries, but in coal mines, tenements, and rural villages. Its power came not only through preaching, but through what Sarah Kreutziger describes as the *"Methodist settlement movement,"* where personal faith overflowed into public transformation. Service, in this view, was not charity—it was sacramental. It was the context in which believers were formed into holy people.

Today, we are reclaiming that legacy. We are rediscovering that mission is not a one-way act of benevolence. It is mutual, embodied, and relational. True Christian service calls us beyond acts of charity into practices of solidarity.

"Standing in the Margin", a framework for multiracial and interclass ministry, reminds us that discipleship includes a commitment to justice and presence. We do not serve from a place of superiority. We serve *alongside*—often in unfamiliar or uncomfortable places—learning from those we thought we came to help. And in doing so, we are shaped by the very people we serve.

This is the school of the Spirit. In this school, we do not simply learn how to act—we learn how to *be*: more humble, more courageous, more compassionate. In service, the fruit of the Spirit begins to take root and grow in us: *love, joy, peace, patience, kindness, generosity, faithfulness, gentleness, and self-control* (Galatians 5:22–23). It is in this shared journey that we are sanctified—not by isolation, but by love in action.

Conclusion: Becoming the Answer to Our Own Prayers

Service is not an extracurricular activity in the Christian life. It is the outward expression of inward grace. It is the lived fulfillment of our baptismal vows—to resist evil, to do good, and to remain in love with God.

When we serve, we are not simply imitating Christ—we are participating in His ongoing mission. We become co-laborers in the kingdom of God. We embody our theology. We enact our prayers. As John Wesley wrote in *The Good Steward*, "All that we have and all that we are is a sacred trust, given for the flourishing of others."

In a culture that elevates consumption and rewards individual achievement, the Church offers a counter-witness: a people shaped by service, formed by love, and sent in grace. We do not serve to be seen. We serve to be changed.

As people of faith, we should often remind ourselves: the goal is not just to *do* church—it is to *be* the Church. Not simply to *host* mission projects—but to become a mission-shaped people. This is how we become the answer to our own prayers: not by waiting passively for God to move, but by joining God where God is already at work.

So we go—forward in service. Not as saviors, but as servants. Not with all the answers, but with open hands and open hearts. And as we give ourselves away, we find that we are drawn deeper into the mystery of grace.

Let us then walk humbly with our God. Let us do justice, love mercy, and serve with joy.

A Blessing (based on Micah 6:8)

Beloved of God,
You already know what is good.
So walk humbly—not in your own strength, but in the Spirit's power.
Love mercy—with the wide generosity that flows from grace.
Do justice—not with clenched fists, but with open hands and a heart ablaze.
And in all things, may you become the answer to your own prayers.
In the name of the One who served us first—Jesus Christ. Amen.

> **IN THE SAME WAY, LET YOUR LIGHT SHINE BEFORE PEOPLE, SO THEY CAN SEE THE GOOD THINGS YOU DO AND PRAISE YOUR FATHER WHO IS IN HEAVEN.**
>
> MATTHEW 5:16, CEB

PART 6
WITNESS
Sharing Our Faith Boldly

Introduction

Christian witness is the visible overflow of an inward transformation—discipleship that shines, not for spectacle, but for the sake of the world God deeply loves.

The vow of *witness* anchors our discipleship in visibility. It reminds us that the Christian life is not intended to be hidden away or practiced in private isolation. To follow Jesus is to be seen—radiantly, courageously, and consistently. In a world increasingly skeptical of institutional religion but still hungry for meaning, discipleship must take shape in public ways. This is not about performative righteousness or forced evangelism, but about living a life so saturated with God's love that others are drawn to the light.

In the Gospel of Matthew, Jesus proclaims, "You are the light of the world" (Matt. 5:14), and then issues the imperative: "Let your light shine before others." This is not a suggestion for the spiritually elite or a calling reserved for clergy; it is the shared vocation of all who claim Christ. Our lives as followers of Christ are to be a beacon—sometimes bright and obvious,

ROOTED IN DISCIPLESHIP

sometimes gentle and persistent, but no matter what, always present. The light we carry is not our own. It is a reflection of the One who is the light of the world, Jesus Christ (John 8:12). Witness, then, is not self-promotion but divine illumination in human transformation.

John Wesley once said, "The world is my parish,"[57] a phrase that radically reoriented the practice of evangelism. No longer confined to church walls or structured services, evangelism was reframed as embodied mission in the public square, the home, the field, and the mines.

Wesley understood witness not only as a theological necessity but also as a spiritual gift—a manifestation of grace extending beyond the self.[58] His commitment to field preaching and to forming disciples in bands and classes demonstrated a vision of witness that was intensely personal yet profoundly communal. For Wesley, witness flowed out of one's assurance of salvation, producing holy living and loving action that could not help but spill over into the world.[59]

The vow of witness, as expressed in the United Methodist Church's baptismal and membership covenant, is a response to the commission of the risen Christ: "You will be my witnesses" (Acts 1:8). This commissioning is not optional. It is the Spirit-empowered call to testify—to tell the truth about what God has done, is doing, and will do. Witness is the natural overflow of grace received. It is both response and responsibility. It is offered in humility and hope, not with the pressure of perfection but with the joy of participation in God's redeeming work.

As people of faith, we recognize that witness cannot be reduced to a program or campaign. It is a culture, a calling, and a spiritual practice. We are forming people who not only *know* the good news but also *show* it—through lives of generosity, compassion, joy, and justice. The vow of witness is not simply about talking louder. It is about living truer. It is about trusting that our lives, when yielded to Christ, become a visible sign of an invisible grace.

Our understanding of witness must empower us to live into this vow not out of fear or obligation, but as an expression of love and trust in the One who sends us.

What does it look like to let our light shine before others in ways that are faithful, personal, and public? How can the Church equip believers to bear witness not just in moments of proclamation, but in the ordinary rhythms of life? As people of faith, we believe that witness is woven into every aspect of

WITNESS

discipleship—from how we speak about our faith, to how we live it out, to how we come together as a community to shine Christ's light in the world.

REFLECTION QUESTIONS:

- ➢ When you reflect on sharing your faith with others, what comes up for you?
- ➢ What might be giving you courage, or what fears might be present in this area?
- ➢ How do your everyday actions reflect your faith?
- ➢ What do you sense God inviting you to explore as your life bears witness to Christ's love?
- ➢ What do you feel when you think about the way your life might be a testimony to others?
- ➢ How might God be calling you to live fully into your witness, both in word and deed?

Sharing Our Faith – The Verbal Witness

The Power of Testimony

Evangelism, at its heart, is the sacred task of telling the good news. It is rooted in the Greek word *euangelion*, meaning "good message" or "good announcement." But for many, the word "evangelism" evokes discomfort or even suspicion. In contemporary culture—and even in the Church—it has been burdened by the weight of past misuses: coercion rather than compassion, colonization instead of communion, and persuasion more than presence. The damage of manipulative or politicized evangelism has created spiritual wounds, particularly in marginalized communities. To recover a faithful practice of witness, we must return to its relational and grace-centered core.

In the Wesleyan tradition, evangelism is not about controlling outcomes but about bearing faithful witness to God's activity in our lives.[60] Methodist historian, theologian, and pastor Albert Outler once described evangelism as "the outward form of inward grace,"[61] a phrase that captures both the simplicity and the power of testimony. In this sense, verbal witness is not transactional—it is incarnational. It flows from our lived encounter with God's love and carries with it the vulnerability, humility, and joy of a person changed by grace. We do not speak of Christ because we have all the answers; we speak of Christ because we have been found.

ROOTED IN DISCIPLESHIP

In the early Methodist movement, testimony was central to communal life.[62] Class meetings regularly included moments where individuals shared how God had been present in their struggles, joys, temptations, and triumphs. This wasn't spiritual performance; it was confession, celebration, and connection. Through these verbal exchanges, members were strengthened in faith and drawn into deeper accountability. Testimony was not merely private reflection—it was public discipleship.

Telling our story is one of the most personal and profound ways we can share Christ. Our stories do not need to be dramatic to be powerful. A quiet word about God's faithfulness in grief, a memory of transformation through prayer, or the simple confession of ongoing struggle accompanied by hope—these are all acts of evangelism. They proclaim not a polished gospel but a present and personal one.

Reflection Questions:

- ➢ When you hear the word *evangelism*, what feelings or experiences come to mind?
- ➢ Have you ever been impacted—positively or negatively—by someone's faith story? What made it memorable?
- ➢ How does the Wesleyan understanding of testimony as "the outward form of inward grace" reshape how you think about sharing your faith?
- ➢ What does it mean to you that verbal witness is *incarnational* and not *transactional*?

Witness as Invitation

Verbal witness is rooted in invitation. We do not demand or impose; we extend an open hand. The language of witness is always framed by love and hospitality: "Would you like to come to church with me?" "Can I tell you what this means to me?" "Can I pray for you?"

These are not manipulative strategies but grace-filled gestures that open the door for deeper encounter. The Spirit often moves through these small openings, planting seeds that grow over time.

The Gospels are filled with simple invitations: "Come and see" (John 1:39), "Follow me" (Matt. 4:19), "Go and tell" (Mark 5:19). Jesus himself models invitational ministry, engaging people in conversation, asking questions, sharing meals, and allowing space for curiosity. He does not force belief; he

WITNESS

cultivates relationship. Verbal witness today, especially in a pluralistic and sometimes suspicious culture, must echo this same invitational posture.

For many, the idea of verbal evangelism conjures images of cold calls or uncomfortable door-to-door visits. But in a Wesleyan understanding, witness is not about confrontation—it's about connection. It begins not with answers, but with listening. Before we speak, we listen to the pain, longings, and hopes of our neighbors. Before we explain doctrine, we honor stories. In doing so, we make space for the Spirit to speak through us, often in ways we did not expect.

Evangelism becomes especially potent in the context of authentic relationships. In workplaces, neighborhoods, schools, and coffee shops, we bear witness not by shouting over people but by walking alongside them. The early church grew not through mass marketing but through networks of relationship, hospitality, and care.[63] People came to faith not because they were argued into belief, but because they encountered Christians whose lives and words bore the unmistakable imprint of Christ's love.[64]

REFLECTION QUESTIONS:

> ➢ Think of a time someone invited you into something meaningful—church, prayer, conversation. What made that invitation feel authentic?
> ➢ How do you typically invite others into faith conversations? What feels natural, and what feels intimidating?
> ➢ Which invitation from the Gospels ("Come and see," "Follow me," or "Go and tell") most resonates with your current season of discipleship? Why?
> ➢ How can your own witness be more rooted in relationship rather than persuasion?

Cultivating Confidence Through Practice

As followers of Christ, we must be committed to helping disciples grow in their ability to share their faith with authenticity and confidence. We must recognize that for many people, verbal witness is intimidating. Some worry they don't know enough Scripture.

Others fear saying the wrong thing. Still others hesitate because they feel their story isn't "powerful" enough. Our response to these concerns is grounded in grace: we do not witness because we are experts—we witness because we are recipients of grace.

ROOTED IN DISCIPLESHIP

To nurture a culture of confident and compassionate witness, we must provide a variety of opportunities for testimony training and story-sharing:

> **Faith Story Workshops:** Periodic gatherings where individuals reflect on how God has worked in their lives and learn to share their story in a three-minute, ten-minute, or written format. These are designed for personal clarity, not performance.

> **Small Group Integration:** Each discipleship groups can include regular space for personal storytelling, allowing members to practice articulating their faith in a safe and supportive environment.

> **Worship and Testimony:** During certain worship services or sermon series, laypeople can be invited to share brief testimonies, modeling vulnerability and reinforcing the idea that witness is for *everyone*, not just pastors or extroverts.

> **One-to-One Discipleship:** Mentorship model can include simple, reproducible tools that help people talk about their spiritual journey. Questions such as "Where have you seen God this week?" or "What has God been teaching you lately?" help normalize spiritual conversation.

These practices demystify witness. They show that verbal evangelism is not an exceptional calling for a few bold believers—it is a natural expression of a growing relationship with Christ. And they reinforce the idea that our faith story, however ordinary it may seem to us, is extraordinary in the hands of the Holy Spirit.

Reflection Questions:

> In what ways have you practiced listening as part of your witness? What did you learn?

> Where in your daily life (workplace, neighborhood, family, etc.) do you have opportunities to walk alongside others as a witness?

> What might it look like for your life and words to carry "the unmistakable imprint of Christ's love"?

> What are your biggest hesitations or fears when it comes to verbal witness?

> Do you feel confident sharing your faith story in 2–3 minutes? Why or why not?

> How has someone else's vulnerability in testimony helped you grow in faith?

- Which of the following practices do you think would help you grow as a witness?
    - Faith story workshops
    - Small group storytelling
    - Worship testimonies
    - One-to-one discipleship
    - Why?

The Verbal Witness as Ministry of Presence

It is important to note that verbal witness does not always involve quoting Scripture or naming Jesus explicitly in every conversation. Sometimes, the most faithful verbal witness is a word of compassion, encouragement, or affirmation. It is the tone of our voice when someone is suffering, the prayer we offer even if it is unspoken, the naming of hope when despair is thick in the air.

In a post-Christian context, verbal witness often functions as pre-evangelism—a gentle articulation of values and convictions that eventually point toward Christ. Over time, as relationships deepen, these moments open doors to more direct conversations about faith. This process is slow, intentional, and Spirit-led. It honors the dignity of the person and the sovereignty of God's timing.

Our task is not to script conversations. It is to remain faithfully present, attuned to the Spirit, and ready to speak when the time is right. This is why prayer is central to verbal witness. We pray not only for boldness to speak, but also for discernment to know when *not* to. We trust that God is always at work ahead of us, and that our words—no matter how simple—can be vessels of divine grace.

Reflection Questions:
- Have you ever offered a word of witness without using explicitly religious language? What happened?
- How might your presence, tone, or compassion be a form of verbal witness?
- What spiritual practices help you become more attentive to the Spirit's prompting in conversations?
- When have you felt the Spirit nudge you to speak—or not to speak? What did you learn from that experience?
- What is one part of your story that you feel led to share with someone in the coming weeks?

- ➢ Who is someone in your life right now who might need a word of witness, encouragement, or hope?
- ➢ How are you praying for opportunities to share Christ—not through pressure, but through presence?

Living Out Our Faith: The Embodied Witness

More Than Words

Matthew 5:16 does *not* say, "So they may hear your sermons," but "So they may see your good works and give glory to your Father in heaven." This subtle yet profound shift reframes our understanding of witness. The emphasis is not on what we say, but on what is seen in our lives. The biblical witness is deeply visual and experiential. From the prophetic signs in the Old Testament to the parables Jesus acted out, the gospel is a story not just to be told but to be embodied.

This is why witness is not limited to pulpits or podiums. It is enacted in the mundane, daily decisions of life—how we treat a server at a restaurant, how we respond to a co-worker in crisis, how we offer time to a neighbor in need. Each moment holds the potential for grace to be revealed.

Witness is incarnational theology made local. The Word became flesh and dwelled *among* us (John 1:14). So too are we called to dwell *among* others, bringing Christ's love near through our presence and participation in the life of the world.

The evangelist and historian Michael Green reminds us that Christianity spread in its earliest centuries not primarily through professional preachers but through what he calls "invisible messengers."[65] These were everyday believers—merchants, servants, mothers, soldiers—who, through their integrity, compassion, and hope, stirred curiosity and invited conversation. They lived in such a way that their lives begged the question: *"Why do you live like this?"*

The goal of Christian witness is not to impress, but to embody. It is a way of life that provokes curiosity, draws people toward Christ, and gives glory to God. When our witness is sincere, rooted in love, and consistent with the gospel, it becomes a luminous presence in a world of shadows.

Holiness as Public Practice

John Wesley's theology of sanctification offers a vital corrective to the modern temptation to privatize faith. For Wesley, holiness was never merely a

WITNESS

personal pursuit—it was inherently social. He famously insisted that "there is no holiness but social holiness."⁶⁶ This meant that the journey of growing in grace required community, accountability, and public expression.

Holiness, in the Wesleyan tradition, finds expression in acts of mercy, justice, hospitality, and generosity. These are not secondary to the gospel—they are integral to it. A holy life, in the Wesleyan tradition, is not confined to the private disciplines of prayer and worship, though these are essential. Rather, holiness expresses itself through active love of neighbor, the pursuit of peace, reconciliation across divides, and the building of communities marked by compassion and justice. For John Wesley, holiness was never merely about withdrawal from the world, but about engagement with it—especially in service to the poor, the oppressed, and the forgotten. True sanctification manifests not only in spiritual devotion but in public acts of mercy and justice that reflect the character of Christ.⁶⁷

As followers of Christ, our discipleship must be practical and visible. Our discipleship pathways are intentionally designed to help people reflect on how their daily habits, relationships, and responsibilities become arenas of witness. From the break room to the classroom, from committee meetings to community organizing, we are called to show forth the fruit of the Spirit: love, joy, peace, patience, kindness, goodness, faithfulness, gentleness, and self-control (Galatians 5:22–23).

In congregational settings, small groups and ministry teams serve not only as venues for spiritual formation but also as laboratories for practicing grace under pressure. When we forgive someone who has hurt us, when we advocate for someone who has been overlooked, when we refuse to retaliate but choose love instead—we are bearing witness.

From Sunday to Everyday: Discipleship That Moves

Too often, witness is mistaken for a moment—something we "do" on a mission trip or during a testimony night. Christian witness, is not a singular event; it is a sustained movement. It is the movement of a life continually conformed to Christ, a faith that seeps into the details of everyday living.

Wesley called this process *going on to perfection*—a lifelong journey of becoming more like Christ, not merely in belief but in behavior.⁶⁸ This journey does not end at the church door. It extends into neighborhoods, schools, hospitals, and social media feeds.

ROOTED IN DISCIPLESHIP

People of faith are called to we celebrate and embody the rhythms of *gathering and scattering*. We gather to worship, to be nourished by Word and Sacrament, to be reminded of God's grace. But we scatter to be broken and shared, just as Christ's body was, for the sake of the world. Our witness happens at the intersection of faith and the ordinary, where the practices of grace shape how we:

- Speak in difficult conversations
- Choose how to spend money
- Parent and partner
- Forgive and ask for forgiveness
- Care for creation
- Seek justice and mercy

Our public witness must be recognizable not just in our church activities but in our everyday ethics.

The Table as Testimony

Our Wesleyan theology reminds us that Holy Communion is more than a means of personal renewal—it is also a missional act.69 When we come to the table, we receive Christ's love poured out "for us and for the world." In that sacred act of receiving, we are reminded of our identity as the Body of Christ—and in being sent forth, we are commissioned to live Eucharistically, becoming what we have received. To live Eucharistically is to allow the grace we encounter at the table to shape the rhythm of our lives beyond it. Just as the bread is taken, blessed, broken, and given, so too are we, as Christ's Body in the world.

Living Eucharistically means embracing a life that mirrors the mystery we receive in Holy Communion. It means allowing ourselves to be taken—claimed by God in love; blessed—affirmed in our belovedness and equipped with spiritual gifts; broken—not in despair, but in vulnerability and humility for the sake of others; and given—offered in service, compassion, and witness to a hurting world. This is not a private spirituality but a public vocation. It transforms the way we eat, serve, relate, and respond to the needs around us.

When we live Eucharistically, we see every shared meal as a sign of hospitality, every act of justice as a foretaste of God's reign, and every welcome extended as an echo of Christ's invitation. We begin to understand that the sacrament does not end with the dismissal—it continues in our daily lives as we become sacraments to others: outward and visible signs of inward and spiritual grace.

WITNESS

To live this way is to proclaim with our lives what we profess in worship: that Christ has died, Christ is risen, and Christ will come again—not just in the sanctuary, but in every place we dare to bear witness through love.

When we cultivate communal practices of hospitality—whether through community meals, potlucks, shared tables, or Sunday fellowship—with evangelistic intentionality, we begin to recognize these gatherings as extensions of the altar. They are not merely social events; they are formative acts of discipleship that embody the Eucharistic life. Each act of welcome, each seat pulled up for someone new, becomes a reflection of the grace we have received and now extend.

These practices shape a people who understand that the sacrament is never self-contained. Grace is never hoarded; it is always shared. When we gather in love, serve one another, and make space for those who are often overlooked, we do more than offer kindness—we bear witness to Christ's inclusive, reconciling love. Every table becomes a testimony. And in this way, we live as sacraments ourselves: outward and visible signs of the inward and spiritual grace that continues to nourish, transform, and send us into the world.

Practices That Form a Public Faith

The vow of witness is not simply an aspiration to hold in our hearts—it is a calling to embody in our lives. It is not abstract or occasional; it is actionable, daily, and deliberate. Just as athletes train their bodies and musicians rehearse their craft, disciples must cultivate a pattern of life that supports a public, visible faith. Christian witness is not reserved for extraordinary moments. It is formed in the ordinary habits that shape us over time into people whose lives reflect the grace of God we proclaim.

A faithful witness does not happen by accident. It is the fruit of intention, formed through spiritual disciplines and missional habits that align our daily lives with the love and mercy of Christ. These practices do not make us perfect; rather, they make us available—to the Spirit's movement, to our neighbors' needs, and to the ongoing work of transformation within and around us.

Prayerful Discernment:

At the heart of a public faith is attentiveness to God's presence. Prayerful discernment is the daily posture of asking, "Where are you at work, God—and how can I join you?" This simple question shifts our gaze outward. It transforms ordinary routines into sacred possibilities. Whether in the checkout line, at a board meeting, or walking through our neighborhoods, prayerful discernment opens our eyes to the Spirit's invitation to participate in God's ongoing mission.

This practice reminds us that witness is not always something we initiate. Often, it begins by paying attention to what God is already doing—and being willing to respond with humility and courage. As disciples cultivate the habit of listening for God's prompting, they begin to recognize moments of witness in the midst of seemingly mundane life.

Radical Hospitality:

Hospitality is more than good manners or well-set tables. In the Christian tradition, hospitality is holiness. For Wesleyans, holiness is not an abstract ideal but the love of God expressed in acts of mercy and justice. Hospitality—welcoming the stranger, making room for the other—is a practical expression of sanctifying grace and a visible mark of discipleship in the way of holiness.

It is the sacred act of making room—for strangers, for stories, for God's surprising grace. To practice radical hospitality is to intentionally welcome the outsider, the forgotten, the inconvenient, and the overlooked into our lives and homes—not as charity, but as an act of solidarity and kinship.[70]

Jesus' ministry was marked by table fellowship with those who were often excluded—sinners, tax collectors, foreigners, the sick. His witness was inseparable from his welcome. When the Church extends that same welcome today, it bears witness to a God whose love is wide and whose table is open. Hospitality is evangelism through embrace. It says to the world, "You belong, even before you believe."

Storytelling and Testimony:

A public faith requires a voice. It means being able to speak of the hope within us—not with rehearsed scripts, but with honesty, humility, and love. Telling our story is one of the most powerful forms of witness we have. It doesn't require theological degrees or dramatic narratives. It simply requires a willingness to say, "Here's what Christ has done in my life."

Practicing testimony allows disciples to claim their experience of God's grace as part of the larger story of redemption. It gives language to transformation and courage to speak in a world that often silences faith or distorts it. Storytelling also builds bridges. It invites others not into debate but into relationship—one story at a time.

WITNESS

Churches can foster this practice by making space for people to share their stories in small groups, worship services, and informal gatherings. As testimony becomes normalized in a community, the fear around evangelism begins to fade. Witness becomes less about persuading and more about sharing what is real.

Compassionate Presence:

Sometimes the most profound witness is simply being there. In moments of grief, loss, anxiety, or transition, words often fall short. But presence—real, unhurried, and attentive presence—speaks volumes. Compassionate presence means showing up for others, especially in times of suffering, without needing to fix, explain, or preach. It is the ministry of listening, of holding space, of carrying burdens with others in love.

This kind of witness echoes the incarnation. Just as God entered into human experience in the person of Jesus, so we are called to enter into the experiences of our neighbors. When we do, we proclaim—without even speaking—that no one is alone, and that God's love shows up in embodied ways. Presence becomes a sacrament, revealing the nearness of the divine through human companionship.

Justice-Seeking Love:

Christian witness must also be prophetic. It must speak to and act within the systems that harm, exclude, and oppress. Justice-seeking love is not an optional extension of faith—it is its core expression. As the prophets declare and Jesus exemplifies, God's heart is always turned toward the marginalized, the vulnerable, the voiceless.

To bear witness in this way is to advocate for policies and practices that reflect the values of God's Kingdom: dignity, equity, compassion, and peace. It may mean standing alongside the incarcerated, challenging economic injustice, dismantling racism, or caring for creation. These acts of justice are not political stunts; they are theological imperatives rooted in the character of God.

When the Church lives this way—grounded in grace and active in love—it becomes a credible witness. It not only speaks good news but embodies it.

These practices are not flashy or attention-grabbing. They are rarely headline-worthy.[71] But over time, they shape lives that shine. They cultivate a witness that is visible, not for self-glory, but for the glory of God. As these habits take root in communities of faith, they form disciples whose lives give off the light of Christ—faithfully, humbly, and persistently.

ROOTED IN DISCIPLESHIP

And when the watching world sees that light, it does not point back to us. It points forward—to the One who is the source of all light, love, and life.

Reflection Questions:
- Where in your daily life do you sense God calling you to be a visible witness?
- What assumptions have you held about witness that might need reimagining in light of incarnational theology?
- How can you practice "hospitality as holiness" this week—in your home, workplace, or congregation?
- Think of a time when someone's life stirred your spiritual curiosity. What was it about them that revealed Christ to you?
- What spiritual disciplines help you stay grounded in love and grace, especially when bearing witness feels hard or risky?
- How can your small group or ministry community support one another in public, everyday discipleship?
- What tables are you being invited to extend or expand, so others might experience the inclusive love of God?

Community and Global Witness

The Church as Witness

The Church is not merely a gathering place for individual witnesses; it is a witness in and of itself. As the Body of Christ, the Church bears visible testimony to God's redemptive presence in the world. It is a sign, an instrument, and a foretaste of the Kingdom of God—called not only to speak the good news, but to embody it through communal life. Wherever the Church proclaims justice, practices reconciliation, cultivates joy, and nurtures peace, it becomes a living signpost of the reign of Christ.

This means that congregational life—its rhythms, priorities, and public witness—matters deeply. When a local church advocates for the poor, builds relationships with civic leaders, welcomes immigrants, supports education, or creates space for the arts, it offers more than good works. It becomes a testimony: that God is not distant but near, not indifferent but invested. Such ministries are not mere charity—they are mission. They proclaim, through presence and practice, that the Church is paying attention, standing alongside, and laboring with its community for the sake of the common good.

The local church's public liturgy also plays a critical role. Worship in the public square, prayer vigils in response to community trauma, and open celebrations of God's goodness make faith visible. These actions say to the world, "We believe God is active here, among us." Even more quietly, the ethos of a congregation—its hospitality, its relationships across difference, its posture toward the vulnerable—can become a profound expression of witness.

Churches must ask themselves regularly: What do our neighbors know about God because of our presence here? Do our ministries reflect the mercy and justice of Jesus? Does our community miss us when we're not around? These are not merely programmatic questions; they are theological ones that speak to the Church's vocation as a visible body of Christ.

In the end, the Church's witness is not measured by its size, visibility, or cultural influence, but by its faithfulness to the way of Jesus. To be the Church is to embody the good news in tangible, consistent, and communal ways. It is to live so rooted in God's love that the surrounding community cannot help but notice. The takeaway is simple and profound: when the Church shows up with compassion, humility, courage, and joy, it becomes a sacrament of God's presence in the world. Let every congregation, no matter its size or setting, ask not how to be successful, but how to be faithful witnesses to the love, justice, and holiness of Christ. This is our calling—and our witness to the world.

Global Mission and Missional Thinking

Christian witness does not stop at neighborhood boundaries. It extends across nations, cultures, and contexts. The global Church bears witness to a God who so loved the *world*—not just a region or tribe.[72] Thus, to be faithful witnesses in our own context, we must also remain attuned to the needs and voices of the worldwide body of Christ.

Global witness includes mission partnerships, cross-cultural relationships, shared learning, and acts of solidarity. When a church supports clean water initiatives in Africa, disaster recovery in the Caribbean, theological education in South America, or peace building in Southeast Asia, it participates in the larger narrative of God's healing work across the globe.

In these acts, the Church becomes a vessel of God's mercy and justice, witnessing to a gospel that is both local and global, both incarnational and expansive. This is not about exporting Western expressions of faith but about mutual transformation and shared discipleship.

Such work requires a shift in imagination. Missional thinking invites churches to see themselves not as isolated outposts but as interconnected communities in the body of Christ.[73] One way to foster this vision is through what some call *glocal* thinking: an awareness that our local practices are always connected to global realities. The food we serve at community meals, the voices we lift in prayer, the policies we advocate for—they all intersect with wider systems of justice and injustice. As Wesleyan Christians, we believe grace is always moving outward—personal holiness gives rise to social holiness, and social holiness extends beyond borders. Recognizing this connection helps us witness with greater humility, integrity, and depth.

The Church's global witness is also sustained through prayer. When congregations pray for believers in other parts of the world—especially those who are persecuted, displaced, or suffering—they proclaim a gospel that transcends borders. When they support missionaries, connect with sister churches, or celebrate the global diversity of Pentecost Sunday, they give witness to the Spirit who is always drawing people from "every nation, tribe, people and language" (Rev. 7:9).

Mission, then, is not a special interest or committee—it is a calling shared by every disciple and every congregation. It is the Church's participation in the missio Dei—the mission of God—who sends the Son, the Spirit, and the Church for the life of the world.[74] It asks us to be attuned to the world God so loves, and to participate boldly and humbly in God's redemptive work both near and far.

Public Faith in the Public Square

Christian witness must also take seriously the vocation of presence in civic life. When churches partner with schools, community organizers, public health workers, or elected leaders—not for political gain, but for the flourishing of all—they embody a public faith that refuses to be privatized. This kind of faith does not seek control, but contributes to the common good. It reflects the conviction that "there is no holiness but social holiness"—an understanding that faith must shape how we engage in the public square.

To be a public Church is not to be partisan. It is to be principled—grounded in the gospel and open to the Spirit's leading. In this way, congregations bear witness not only by what they say or do in church buildings, but by how they stand in the community as agents of reconciliation, compassion, and hope.

WITNESS

The Church's presence in the world is not primarily about influence or authority; it is about truth-telling through the character of its life together. Communities of faith must embody alternative patterns of relationship, economy, and care that contrast with the false narratives of fear, individualism, and competition. The public role of the Church is not to mirror society's divisions but to offer a foretaste of God's justice and joy made visible in everyday practices of peace and mutual care.[75] As Martin Luther King Jr. once wrote, the Church must not be "a thermometer that recorded the ideas and principles of popular opinion," but "a thermostat that transformed the mores of society," serving as the moral conscience of the world through its courageous witness and faithful presence.[76]

Throughout history, Christians have understood that spiritual transformation and public engagement are inseparable. Early Methodists visited prisons, opposed economic injustice, and organized to alleviate suffering—not to earn salvation but as the fruit of it. This tradition continues when churches resist domination, challenge exploitative systems, and participate in movements that promote equity and dignity. Public faith becomes real when congregations recognize that what they pray, preach, and practice locally is shaped by—and shapes—the larger systems in which they live.[77]

To live this way is to resist both privatized religion and politicized religion. It is to take the long road of faithful presence, listening deeply, speaking wisely, and acting justly. A public faith is not a performance—it is a disciplined and hope-filled practice, grounded in the life of the crucified and risen Christ, who is Lord of all.

To help congregations embody this vision, churches might consider the following practical steps:

> - Host community listening sessions where neighbors, especially those on the margins, are invited to share concerns, hopes, and dreams.
> - Appoint or support a justice ministry team to monitor local civic issues, identify opportunities for partnership, and lead the congregation in advocacy.
> - Develop long-term partnerships with public schools, health clinics, and grassroots organizations—not merely as service projects, but as mutual relationships grounded in shared well-being.
> - Make space in worship for public prayer that names local and global injustices, intercedes for public servants, and affirms the dignity of all people.

ROOTED IN DISCIPLESHIP

- ➤ Use church property as public commons—hosting community gardens, free pantries, town halls, or cultural events that foster connection and belonging.
- ➤ Equip members for public discipleship through small group studies on Christian ethics, economic justice, and civic engagement grounded in Scripture and Wesleyan theology.
- ➤ Commit to visible, humble presence at public demonstrations or prayer vigils that respond to violence, racism, or environmental degradation—practicing non-anxious witness rather than triumphalism.
- ➤ Build relationships across faith traditions and political perspectives, modeling Christ-centered hospitality and dialogue in a polarized world.

By engaging in these practices, the Church lives into its vocation as a public body of grace—one that does not retreat from the world's challenges, but leans into them with faith, hope, and love.

A Structure of Nurture, Outreach, and Witness

Discipleship should encompass all aspects of our lives, growth and missional engagement. Each component—Nurture, Outreach, and Witness—reflects the holistic nature of our church's life and the call to grow as disciples in every area of life. Here's how each area provides tangible ways for you to live out your vows of prayers, presence, gifts, service, and witness.

Nurture: Growing Together in Faith

- ➤ **Bible Studies and Small Groups:** Joining a Bible study or small group is one of the best ways to connect with others and grow deeper in your faith. Whether you are looking for a group based on life stage, interest, or spiritual focus, church has a place for you. These gatherings are designed to be spaces where you can learn, ask questions, and find support from fellow disciples. They embody the vow of presence by encouraging consistent participation and mutual care.
- ➤ **Prayer Gatherings and Retreats:** Discipleship begins with being nurtured in our connection with God. We offer regular prayer gatherings, such as our midweek prayer service, and annual retreats to foster personal spiritual growth. These gatherings allow us to practice our vow of prayers and seek God's guidance together.

WITNESS

> **Fellowship Events:** Opportunities for fellowship—whether through Sunday coffee hours, church picnics, or special intergenerational worship services—nurture our relationships and allow us to practice hospitality, embodying our commitment to presence and service. These moments build a sense of community where every member feels welcome and valued.

Ways to Get Involved:
> Join a Sunday School class or small group.
> Attend our monthly prayer gatherings and seek God's direction for our church and community.
> Participate in fellowship events that strengthen the bonds within our church family.

Outreach: Serving Beyond Ourselves

> **Local Mission Projects:** The outreach ministries of the local church are a direct response to the Christian call to serve. Throughout the year, congregations partner with community organizations to meet the needs of their neighbors through acts of compassion and justice. Opportunities for involvement may include food drives, service projects, and other hands-on ministries that allow disciples to embody the love of Christ in tangible ways.

> **Global Mission Trips:** Discipleship is not confined to a single place or context; it extends to the whole world. Many churches engage in global mission work through international partnerships, financial support, and mission trips. These efforts provide opportunities for individuals and communities to live out the Great Commission—bearing witness to Christ's love in diverse and far-reaching places.

> **Community Partnerships:** Many congregations collaborate with local agencies to respond to the needs of their communities. Whether supporting meal programs, mentoring initiatives, or advocating for justice, these partnerships extend the church's outreach and provide practical ways to serve as witnesses to Christ's love and compassion.

ROOTED IN DISCIPLESHIP

Ways to Get Involved:
- ➤ Sign up for a local mission project or consider joining a mission trip abroad.
- ➤ Volunteer with one of our community partners, offering your gifts and service to those in need.
- ➤ Explore how your unique skills can contribute to outreach efforts, whether through advocacy, hands-on service, or financial support.

Witness: Sharing God's Love

- ➤ **Evangelism and Invitation:** Evangelism and invitation are vital expressions of Christian witness. Churches can equip individuals to share their faith with authenticity and confidence in everyday relationships—with friends, family, neighbors, and colleagues. Congregational outreach events also create welcoming spaces where others can encounter the love of God through a supportive and grace-filled community.
- ➤ **Sharing Your Story:** Each of us has a story of how God's grace has impacted our lives. Witnessing isn't just about words—it's about living a life that reflects Christ's love. By sharing your personal story of faith with others, you can offer hope and invite them to explore a relationship with God.
- ➤ **Community Witness Events:** Throughout the year, churches host events that create space for the wider community to experience God's love—whether through seasonal celebrations, worship services, or outreach initiatives. These gatherings offer meaningful opportunities to extend hospitality and invite others to encounter the life-giving presence of Christ through the local church.

Ways to Get Involved:
- ➤ Attend our evangelism workshops and grow in confidence to share your faith.
- ➤ Invite a friend or neighbor to church or to a special community event.
- ➤ Pray for those in your life who may need to experience God's love through you.

A Journey for Every Generation

Discipleship is a lifelong journey for all ages. Our faith calls us to engage children, youth, adults, and seniors, recognizing that we grow best when we serve alongside one another and learn from each generation's wisdom and energy.

Opportunities for Every Age:

- **Children's Ministry:** Our Sunday School and Vacation Bible School programs provide age-appropriate discipleship for children, helping them learn about Jesus in a fun, engaging way. From singing in children's choir to participating in mission projects, our youngest disciples are invited to grow in their faith from an early age.
- **Youth Ministry:** Middle and high school students are invited into deeper discipleship through weekly youth group, mission trips, and small groups that encourage them to ask questions and grow in their faith. Special retreats and confirmation classes also help them explore their calling to follow Jesus.
- **Adult and Senior Ministries:** For adults and seniors, there are abundant opportunities to grow as disciples through small groups, Bible studies, and service initiatives. Whether seeking to deepen spiritual life, take on leadership roles, or mentor younger generations, individuals are invited to engage in meaningful ways that nurture faith and foster spiritual maturity within the life of the church.

GLOSSARY

Baptism

Baptism is a sacred act where we are welcomed into the family of God. It symbolizes the washing away of sin and our new life in Christ. For United Methodists, baptism is not just about our decision to follow Jesus, but also about God's grace reaching out to us, marking us as beloved children of God.

Church

More than a building or service, 'Church' refers to the gathered and scattered body of Christ. In this project, the Church is understood as the community that forms, supports, and sends disciples, embodying God's grace in the world.

Communion

Communion, also called the Lord's Supper, is a sacred meal where we remember Jesus' sacrifice for us on the cross. In this meal, we eat bread and drink from the cup, symbolizing Jesus' body and blood given for us. Through Communion, we experience God's grace and are united with Christ and one another in a special way.

GLOSSARY

Conversion

Conversion is the moment or process when a person turns toward God, deciding to follow Jesus and trust in Him for salvation. It involves a change of heart and mind, where we leave behind our old ways and embrace a new life centered on God's love and purpose.

Disciple

A disciple is someone who chooses to follow Jesus Christ, learning from His teachings and seeking to live a life that reflects His love, grace, and compassion. Being a disciple is about growing in faith and becoming more like Jesus in how we love God and serve others.

Discipleship

Discipleship is the lifelong journey of growing in faith and relationship with Jesus. It involves learning, practicing spiritual disciplines, and living out our faith by loving and serving others. Discipleship is how we continually grow in our understanding of God and His call for us to live as followers of Christ.

Discipleship System

A discipleship system is an intentional and organized plan that helps guide individuals and communities through the process of spiritual growth and faith formation. It creates pathways for people of all ages to deepen their relationship with Jesus, whether they are new to faith or have been following Christ for many years.

Discipling Process

The discipling process is the step-by-step journey of helping someone grow in their relationship with Jesus. It includes teaching, mentoring, encouragement, and providing opportunities for service and spiritual practice, all with the goal of helping each person mature in their faith.

Faith Journey

A faith journey is the ongoing path we walk as we grow in our relationship with God. It includes moments of learning, struggle, joy, and discovery. Each person's faith journey is unique, but it is always about moving toward a deeper understanding of God's love and purpose for our lives.

ROOTED IN DISCIPLESHIP

Gifts

Gifts are the talents, resources, time, and spiritual graces that each person brings to the life of the church. Discerning and offering these gifts is a vital part of Methodist discipleship and communal flourishing.

Means of Grace

The means of grace are the ways God's love and presence come to us, helping us grow spiritually. These include practices like prayer, reading Scripture, taking Communion, serving others, and participating in worship. They are gifts that help us draw closer to God and live out our faith in everyday life.

Prayer

Prayer is talking with God. It is a way we can share our thoughts, hopes, fears, and joys with God, and also a way to listen for His guidance. Through prayer, we build our relationship with God, trusting that He hears us, loves us, and is always with us.

Psalm / Psalms / The Psalms

The Psalms are more than Scripture—they are prayers, laments, and songs that teach us how to relate honestly to God. This project uses the Psalms as a foundational spiritual practice, especially within the vow of prayer.

Reflection / Reflection Questions

Reflection in this project is a spiritual discipline that encourages deep engagement with Scripture, experience, and community. Reflection Questions serve as tools for spiritual growth, small group conversation, and personal formation.

Salvation

Salvation is the gift of being saved by God's grace, through faith in Jesus Christ. It means being rescued from sin and given the promise of eternal life with God. Salvation brings forgiveness, freedom, and a new beginning in our relationship with God.

Scripture

Scripture, while sacred text, is presented in this project as a living guide for prayer, reflection, and practice. It is interpreted within community and serves as one of the primary means of grace.

GLOSSARY

Service

Service is a lived expression of faith that goes beyond volunteerism. It includes acts of compassion, justice, and mercy, reflecting Christ's love in tangible ways. It is one of the core vows of Methodist discipleship.

Small (Groups)

Small groups are the backbone of Methodist formation, rooted in Wesley's class meetings. They provide space for mutual support, accountability, and spiritual growth in community.

Spirit / Holy Spirit

The Holy Spirit is emphasized as the living presence of God, actively participating in the journey of discipleship. It is through the Spirit that transformation, discernment, and empowerment take place.

Spiritual Awakening

Spiritual awakening is a moment of realization or awareness of God's presence and love in a new, profound way. It can be a turning point where we sense God calling us to a deeper, more meaningful relationship with Him. It often leads to renewed faith and a desire to live a life that reflects God's goodness.

Transformation

Transformation is the ongoing change that happens in our lives as we follow Jesus. Through the Holy Spirit, we are continually shaped and molded to become more like Christ—living out love, mercy, and justice in the world. Transformation is about inner renewal and growth in our character and actions.

Wesley / John Wesley / Wesleyan

These terms refer to the theological and practical legacy of John Wesley, co-founder of Methodism. Wesleyan theology emphasizes grace, spiritual discipline, and accountable community, all foundational to this project.

ROOTED IN DISCIPLESHIP

Witness

Witness refers to the outward expression of inward faith. It includes testimony, storytelling, and living a life that reflects the Gospel. It is a commitment to make Christ known through word, action, and presence.

Worship

Worship is the way we express our love, gratitude, and praise to God. It can happen through singing, prayer, reading Scripture, serving others, or simply being still in God's presence. Worship is about giving our hearts to God and recognizing His goodness and greatness.

APPENDIX 1
FAITH STORY WORKSHOP
"Telling Our Story, Sharing God's Grace"

Workshop Overview:

This 2.5-hour workshop invites participants to reflect on and share their personal journeys of faith in a supportive community. Rooted in Scripture and United Methodist theology, the workshop empowers people to articulate their experiences of God's grace and prepare to share those stories as a form of Christian witness.

Goals
- ➢ To help participants recognize God's presence in their lives through reflection and storytelling.
- ➢ To equip participants to share their faith story in personal, communal, and missional contexts.

ROOTED IN DISCIPLESHIP

> ➤ To cultivate a culture of testimony in the church that encourages witness as a spiritual discipline.

Workshop Outline

1. Welcome and Worship (20 minutes)

Scripture Reading: 1 Peter 3:15 (NRSVUE) – "Always be ready to make your defense to anyone who demands from you an accounting for the hope that is in you…"

Hymn: "I Love to Tell the Story" *(UMH 156)*

Prayer: A prayer of openness to the Spirit and a commissioning for courage to share.

2. What is a Faith Story? (15 minutes)

Mini-Teaching: A brief lesson on what constitutes a faith story.

- ➤ Not a perfect story, but a *truthful one.*
- ➤ A witness, not a sermon.
- ➤ Points to God, not to self.
- ➤ Reflects grace, struggle, transformation, and hope.

Quote from John Wesley: "Give me one hundred preachers who fear nothing but sin and desire nothing but God… such alone will shake the gates of hell."[78]

Apply this to *laity* as everyday preachers of grace through story.

3. Story Mapping (30 minutes)

Individual Exercise: Use a guided worksheet with prompts to map out key faith moments:

- ➤ Early spiritual memories
- ➤ People who have shaped your faith
- ➤ Times of doubt or struggle
- ➤ A moment of transformation or deeper commitment
- ➤ Where are you now in your journey?

Optional Worksheet Title: *"The Road So Far…"*

APPENDIX

4. The Power of Testimony (15 minutes)

Video or Live Testimony: Share a short, simple faith story from a trusted church member.

Discussion Questions:
- What stood out to you?
- What made it powerful?
- What did you hear about God?

5. Faith Story Framework (20 minutes)

Simple Model:
- Before: What was your life like before this experience?
- Encounter: How did God meet you in a specific way?
- After: How has your life been changed?

Provide a sample 2-minute story that models clarity and humility.

6. Writing and Practicing (30 minutes)

Guided Time to Write: Encourage participants to write a 2-3 minute version of their story using the framework.

Small Group Practice: Break into groups of 3–4 to practice sharing. Emphasize listening well, offering encouragement, and noting where the Spirit moves.

7. Sending and Sharing (15 minutes)

Reflection: How might God be calling you to share your story—with a neighbor, coworker, or family member?

Prayer of Commissioning: Lay hands or bless each participant to "go and tell."

Take-Home Resource:
- A "Faith Story Toolkit" including:
- A story template
- Ideas for sharing: social media, small groups, mentoring relationships
- Scriptures on witness and storytelling
- A sample prayer for courage

ROOTED IN DISCIPLESHIP

Adaptation Options
- ➢ Youth version: Include drawing, journaling, or video-recording stories.
- ➢ Retreat Setting: Stretch over a weekend with deeper reflection and worship.
- ➢ Sermon Series Tie-in: Pair with a sermon series on *witness* or *telling your story*.

Theological Grounding
This workshop reflects:
- ➢ Wesleyan theology of grace (prevenient, justifying, sanctifying.)
- ➢ Means of Grace: Witness as an outward sign of inward grace.
- ➢ Membership Vow: "To faithfully participate in the church's ministries by... witness"
- ➢ Scriptural Foundation: 1 Peter 3:15, Psalm 107:2, Luke 8:39, Acts 1:8

APPENDIX

Faith Story Toolkit

> *"Let the redeemed of the Lord say so..."*
> — PSALM 107:2 (ESV)

Faith Story Template

Use this simple three-part structure to write your faith story:

1. Before

What was your life like before this moment in your journey?

- ➢ How did you view God, church, or faith?
- ➢ Were you facing a struggle, question, or turning point?

2. Encounter

How did you experience God's grace?

- ➢ Was it through a person, an event, a worship experience, Scripture, prayer, or something unexpected?
- ➢ How did God meet you in that moment?

3. After

How has your life been changed or shaped since that moment?

- ➢ What have you learned about God, yourself, or others?
- ➢ How do you live out your faith differently now?

Aim for a 2–3 minute version. Write it out, speak it aloud, and refine with love.

Ideas for Sharing Your Faith Story

You don't need a microphone or pulpit to tell your story. Try one of these ways:

In Relationships

- ➢ Share your story over coffee with a friend going through a hard time.
- ➢ Use it to start a deeper conversation in a mentoring relationship or small group.
- ➢ Write a letter to your child, godchild, or grandchild with your testimony.

ROOTED IN DISCIPLESHIP

In Ministry
- ➢ Offer to share during worship, a retreat, or confirmation class.
- ➢ Create a 2-minute video testimony for your church's website or social media.
- ➢ Use your story in pastoral care, lay visitation, or community outreach.

In Daily Life
- ➢ Integrate your story into conversations at work or school when appropriate.
- ➢ Post a meaningful reflection or turning point on social media.
- ➢ Share how God has worked in your life during a mission trip or service project.

Scriptures on Witness and Storytelling

Here are a few passages to reflect on as you prepare your story:

- ➢ **1 Peter 3:15 (NIV)** – "Always be prepared to give an answer to everyone who asks you to give the reason for the hope that you have. But do this with gentleness and respect."
- ➢ **Psalm 107:2a (NIRV)** – "Let those who have been set free by the Lord tell their story."
- ➢ **Luke 8:39a (NRSVUE)** – "Return to your home, and declare how much God has done for you."
- ➢ **Acts 1:8 (NIRV)** – "But you will receive power when the Holy Spirit comes on you. Then you will tell people about me in Jerusalem, and in all Judea and Samaria. And you will even tell other people about me from one end of the earth to the other."
- ➢ **John 4:39 (CEB)** – "Many Samaritans in that city believed in Jesus because of the woman's word when she testified."

A Prayer for Courage to Share Your Story

God of grace and truth,
Thank you for walking with me through every season of life.
Give me eyes to see how you have been at work in my story.
When I speak, let it be with humility and love.

APPENDIX

When I listen, help me honor the stories of others.
Grant me courage to testify to your goodness,
and boldness to speak of your grace,
that others may come to know your love through the witness of my life.
In Jesus' name, Amen.

Final Encouragement

Your story may be the light someone else is praying for. Don't underestimate the power of your witness. The Spirit speaks through ordinary people—just like you.

NOTES

Part 1

1. Scott J. Jones, *United Methodist Doctrine: The Extreme Center* (Nashville: Abingdon Press, 2002), 167.
2. Thurman, Howard. *Meditations of the Heart* (p. 90). Beacon Press. Kindle Edition.

Part 2

3. E. Stanley Jones, *How to Pray* (Ravenio Books, 2015), 3.
4. Howard Thurman, Meditations of the Heart (Kindle Locations 264-265). Beacon Press. Kindle Edition.
5. Kathleen Norris, *Amazing Grace: A Vocabulary of Faith,* Riverhead Books; Revised ed. edition (April 1, 1999), 350, 351.
6. Howard Thurman. *Meditations of the Heart* (p. 90). Beacon Press. Kindle Edition.

APPENDIX

7   Tremper Longman III, Psalms: An Introduction and Commentary.

Part 3

8   The United Methodist Church, *This Holy Mystery: A United Methodist Understanding of Holy Communion* (Nashville: General Board of Discipleship, 2004), 7-8, 18.

9   John Wesley, *The Nature, Design, and General Rules of the United Societies* (1743), in John Wesley & Charles Wesley, *Selected Writings and Hymns (Classics of Western Spirituality)*, ed. Frank Whaling (New York: Paulist Press, 1981), 108

10   Frank Whaling, ed., John Wesley and Charles Wesley: Selected Writings and Hymns (New York: Paulist Press, 1981), 63-64.

11   John Wesley, *The Nature, Design, and General Rules of the United Societies* (1743), in *John Wesley and Charles Wesley: Selected Writings and Hymns*, ed. Frank Whaling (New York: Paulist Press, 1981), 108.

12   Frank Whaling, ed., *John Wesley and Charles Wesley: Selected Writings and Hymns*, Classics of Western Spirituality (New York: Paulist Press, 1981), 63.

13   John Wesley, *The Works of John Wesley*, vol. 7, *A Collection of Hymns for the Use of the People Called Methodists*, ed. Franz Hildebrandt and Oliver A. Beckerlegge (Nashville: Abingdon Press, 1983), 74–75.

14   Debra Rienstra and Ron Rienstra, *Worship Words: Discipling Language for Faithful Ministry* (Grand Rapids: Baker Academic, 2009), 44.

15   John Wesley, *The Character of a Methodist* (1742), in *The Works of John Wesley*, vol. 9, ed. Rupert E. Davies (Nashville: Abingdon Press, 1989), 35–40.

16   Ruth C. Duck, *Worship for the Whole People of God: Vital Worship for the 21st Century* (Louisville: Westminster John Knox Press, 2013), 12.

17   *The Book of Worship for Church and Home* (Nashville: United Methodist Publishing House, 1965), 13; cf. Romans 12:1.

18   *This Holy Mystery: A United Methodist Understanding of Holy Communion* (Nashville: General Board of Discipleship of The United Methodist Church, 2004), 10–12.

19 John Wesley, *The Nature, Design, and General Rules of the United Societies* (1743), in *The Works of John Wesley*, vol. 9, ed. Rupert E. Davies (Nashville: Abingdon Press, 1989), 70–73.

20 John Wesley, *The Nature, Design, and General Rules of the United Societies* (1743), in *The Works of John Wesley*, vol. 9, ed. Rupert E. Davies (Nashville: Abingdon Press, 1989), 70–73.

21 Ruth C. Duck, Worship for the Whole People of God: Vital Worship for the 21st Century (Louisville: Westminster John Knox Press, 2013), 12.

22 John Wesley, The Character of a Methodist (1742), in The Works of John Wesley, vol. 9, ed. Rupert E. Davies (Nashville: Abingdon Press, 1989), 35–40.

23 John Wesley and Charles Wesley, *Selected Writings and Hymns*, ed. Frank Whaling (New York: Paulist Press, 1981), 169.

24 John Wesley, "*The Scripture Way of Salvation*," in T*he Works of John Wesley, vol. 1*, ed. Albert C. Outler (Nashville: Abingdon Press, 1984), 274–284.

25 Gayle Carlton Felton, *This Holy Mystery: A United Methodist Understanding of Holy Communion* (Nashville: General Board of Discipleship, 2004), 8.

26 John Wesley, *The Nature, Design, and General Rules of the United Societies (1743)*, in *The Works of John Wesley, vol. 9*, ed. Rupert E. Davies (Nashville: Abingdon Press, 1989), 70–73.

27 Galatians 6:2.

28 John Wesley, *The Nature, Design, and General Rules of the United Societies (1743)*, in *The Works of John Wesley, vol. 9*, ed. Rupert E. Davies (Nashville: Abingdon Press, 1989), 70–73.

29 Kevin M. Watson, *The Class Meeting: Reclaiming a Forgotten (and Essential) Small Group Experience* (Wilmore, KY: Seedbed, 2014), 11–13.

30 John Wesley, *The Nature, Design, and General Rules of the United Societies* (1743), in *The Works of John Wesley*, vol. 9, ed. Rupert E. Davies (Nashville: Abingdon Press, 1989), 70–73.

31 Gayle Carlton Felton, *By Water and the Spirit: Making Connections for Identity and Ministry* (Nashville: Discipleship Resources, 1998), 17.

32 David Lowes Watson, *Accountable Discipleship: Living in God's Household* (Nashville: Discipleship Resources, 1997), 45–48.

APPENDIX

33 John Wesley, *The Duty of Constant Communion, in The Works of John Wesley, vol. 7*, ed. Franz Hildebrandt and Oliver A. Beckerlegge (Nashville: Abingdon Press, 1983), 138–139.

34 Henri J.M. Nouwen, *Out of Solitude: Three Meditations on the Christian Life* (Notre Dame, IN: Ave Maria Press, 1974), 32.

35 David Lowes Watson, *Accountable Discipleship: Living in God's Household* (Nashville: Discipleship Resources, 1997), 84.

Part 4

36 John Wesley, Sermon 51: The Good Steward, in The Works of John Wesley, ed. Albert C. Outler (Nashville: Abingdon, 1986), 2:284.

37 John Wesley, *Sermon 51: The Good Steward*, 2:288.

38 John Wesley, *Sermon 50: The Use of Money*, in *The Works of John Wesley*, ed. Thomas Jackson (Grand Rapids: Baker Book House, 1979), 6:126.

39 Thurman, Howard, "The Sound of the Genuine (Baccalaureate ceremony) (Spelman College), 1980 May 4," *The Howard Thurman Digital Archive*, https://thurman.pitts.emory.edu/items/show/838.

40 John P. Kretzmann and John L. McKnight, *Building Communities from the Inside Out: A Path Toward Finding and Mobilizing a Community's Assets* (ACTA Publications, 1993), 25.

Part 5

41 John Wesley, letter to John Clayton (1739), in *The Works of John Wesley*, vol. 25, ed. Thomas Jackson (Grand Rapids: Baker Book House, 1984), 219.

42 Richard P. Heitzenrater, *Wesley and the People Called Methodists* (Nashville: Abingdon Press, 1995), 234.

43 M. Douglas Meeks, *God the Economist: The Doctrine of God and Political Economy* (Minneapolis: Fortress Press, 1989), 146.

44 M. Douglas Meeks, *God the Economist: The Doctrine of God and Political Economy* (Minneapolis: Fortress Press, 1989), 68.

45 John Wesley, *The Doctrine of Original Sin*, in *The Works of John Wesley*, Vol. 9, ed. Thomas Jackson (Grand Rapids: Baker Book House, 1986), 191.

46 John Wesley, *Sermon 98: On Visiting the Sick*, in *The Works of John Wesley*, Vol. 3, ed. Albert C. Outler (Nashville: Abingdon, 1986), 387–395.

47 Russell E. Richey, *Connectionalism: Ecclesiology, Mission, and Identity, in United Methodism and American Culture: Volume I*, Abingdon Press, 1997, p. 3

48 Kenneth Cain Kinghorn, *John Wesley on Christian Practice: The Standard Sermons in Modern English, Volume III, Sermons 34–53* (Nashville: Abingdon Press, 2003), 11

49 John Wesley, *The Way to the Kingdom*, in *The Works of John Wesley*, vol. 1, ed. Albert C. Outler (Nashville: Abingdon Press, 1984), 225–233.

50 Gwen Purushotham, *Watching Over One Another in Love* (Nashville: General Board of Discipleship, The United Methodist Church, 2006), 8.

51 John Wesley, *Preface to Hymns and Sacred Poems (1739)*, in *The Works of John Wesley*, vol. 13, ed. Paul Wesley Chilcote and Kenneth J. Collins (Nashville: Abingdon Press, 2013), 39

52 John Wesley, *On Zeal*, in *John Wesley on the Christian Practice: The Standard Sermons in Modern English, Vol. 3, Sermons 34–53*, ed. Kenneth Cain Kinghorn (Nashville: Abingdon Press, 2003), 113.

53 *Sent in Love: The United Methodist Church and Ecumenism—A Theological Foundation for Full Communion*, draft report of the Committee on Faith and Order (September 2019), 20.

54 While commonly attributed to John Wesley, this is not found in his published works. See *The United Methodist Handbook* (Nashville: United Methodist Communications, 2016), 7.

55 Anne L. Burkholder and Thomas W. Elliott Jr., *A Quick and Easy Guide to United Methodist Polity* (Nashville: Abingdon Press, 2008), 59–60.

56 John Wesley, *The Journal of John Wesley*, ed. Nehemiah Curnock (London: Epworth Press, 1909), May 24, 1738.

Part 6

57 John Wesley, *The Works of John Wesley, Vol. 19: Journal and Diaries I (1735–1738)*, ed. W. Reginald Ward and Richard P. Heitzenrater (Nashville: Abingdon Press, 1988), 67.

58 Randy L. Maddox, *Responsible Grace: John Wesley's Practical Theology* (Nashville: Kingswood Books, 1994), 192–193.

APPENDIX

59 John Wesley, "The Witness of the Spirit, I," in *The Works of John Wesley*, Vol. 1: *Sermons I, 1–33*, ed. Albert C. Outler (Nashville: Abingdon Press, 1984), 284–297.

60 Randy L. Maddox, *Responsible Grace: John Wesley's Practical Theology* (Nashville: Kingswood Books, 1994), 189–191.

61 Albert C. Outler, "Evangelism in the Wesleyan Spirit," in *Evangelism in the Wesleyan Spirit*, ed. Albert C. Outler (Nashville: Discipleship Resources, 1971), 14.

62 Richard P. Heitzenrater, *Wesley and the People Called Methodists* (Nashville: Abingdon Press, 1995), 164–165.

63 Rodney Stark, *The Rise of Christianity: How the Obscure, Marginal Jesus Movement Became the Dominant Religious Force in the Western World in a Few Centuries* (San Francisco: HarperSanFrancisco, 1997), 129–135.

64 Alan Kreider, *The Patient Ferment of the Early Church: The Improbable Rise of Christianity in the Roman Empire* (Grand Rapids: Baker Academic, 2016), 130.

65 Michael Green, *Evangelism in the Early Church* (Grand Rapids, MI: Eerdmans, 2004), 173.

66 John Wesley, *Preface to Hymns and Sacred Poems (1739)*, in *The Works of John Wesley*, vol. 14, ed. Frank Baker (Nashville: Abingdon Press, 1983), 321.

67 Randy L. Maddox explains that for Wesley, "holiness was essentially a matter of renewing persons in the image of God—which was defined in relational terms: love of God and neighbor." See Randy L. Maddox, *Responsible Grace: John Wesley's Practical Theology* (Nashville: Kingswood Books, 1994), 82.

68 John Wesley, "The Character of a Methodist," in *The Works of John Wesley*, vol. 9, ed. Rupert E. Davies (Nashville: Abingdon Press, 1984), 35–36.

69 Henry H. Knight III, *The Presence of God in the Christian Life: John Wesley and the Means of Grace* (Metuchen, NJ: Scarecrow Press, 1992), 117–19.

70 Christine D. Pohl, *Making Room: Recovering Hospitality as a Christian Tradition* (Grand Rapids, MI: Eerdmans, 1999), 5–6;

71 Howard A. Snyder, *The Radical Wesley and Patterns for Church Renewal* (Downers Grove, IL: IVP Academic, 1980), 129.

72 Christopher J. H. Wright, The Mission of God's People: A Biblical Theology of the Church's Mission (Grand Rapids, MI: Zondervan, 2010), 148.

73 Darrell L. Guder, Missional Church: A Vision for the Sending of the Church in North America (Grand Rapids, MI: Eerdmans, 1998), 82.

74 David J. Bosch, *Transforming Mission: Paradigm Shifts in Theology of Mission* (Maryknoll, NY: Orbis Books, 1991), 390.

75 Stanley Hauerwas, *A Community of Character: Toward a Constructive Christian Social Ethic* (Notre Dame, IN: University of Notre Dame Press, 1981), 42–44.

76 Martin Luther King Jr., *Letter from Birmingham Jail*, April 16, 1963, in *Why We Can't Wait* (New York: New American Library, 1964), 92–93.

77 Joerg Rieger, *No Religion but Social Religion: Liberating Wesleyan Theology* (Nashville, TN: General Board of Higher Education and Ministry, 2008), 56–58.

Appendix 1

78 John Wesley, *The Works of John Wesley*, 3rd ed. (Peabody, MA: Hendrickson Publishers, 2007), 7:101.

www.ingramcontent.com/pod-product-compliance
Lightning Source LLC
Chambersburg PA
CBHW031322160426
43196CB00007B/633